MINI TREKS IN THE NORTH PENNINES

Mini Treks
in the North Pennines

Sheila Gordon

Illustrations & photographs by
Frank Gordon

Carnegie Publishing Ltd

First published in 1999 by
Carnegie Publishing Ltd,
Carnegie House,
Chatsworth Road,
Lancaster LA1 4SL

British Library Cataloguing-in-Publication data
A catalogue record for this book is available from the British Library

ISBN 1-85936-064-5

Typeset and originated by Carnegie Publishing Ltd
Printed and bound by Bookcraft (Bath) Ltd

Contents

*To the memory of all the old lead miners
and especially to 't auld man*

Acknowledgements

Thank you to Frank for all his help both in checking the routes and the text, for the maps and drawings and particularly for his support along the way. Special thanks to Helen for walking the routes with me in all weathers; she always managed to stay cheerful even in the worst of conditions. Thank you also to my sister Lynda for making me a present of *England's Last Wilderness*, a book by David Bellamy and Brendan Quayle which was one of the original inspirations for this book. Its beautifully evocative photographs opened my eyes to the wonders of the North Pennines area.

Disclaimer

Whilst every effort has been made to represent the route accurately in the route description, neither the author nor the publisher can accept any responsibility in connection with any trespass arising from the use of the definitive route or any associated route.

Whilst the author has walked and researched the entire route for the purpose of this guide, no responsibility can be accepted for any unforeseen circumstances encountered while following it.

Preface

Two whole days walking amidst beautiful countryside and learning about the history of the places you visit, with somewhere for a good meal and to lay your head at the end of the day – this is the 'mini treks' concept.

In these often stressful times the idea of a weekend away from it all can act as a panacea, restoring the equilibrium and recharging batteries. To pass those days travelling through the landscape, listening to the sounds of nature, experiencing the peace and tranquility of the hills and valleys, is surely one of the most exquisite ways to spend a weekend. The actual physical process of putting one foot in front of another for mile after mile occupies the body fully, leaving the mind free to wander at will.

Food and drink taste so much better too after a full day in the hills, so a good pub with a warm welcome was a priority for the end of the day. Somewhere to stock up on supplies was also considered essential so that less weight has to be carried in the pack. For the backpackers amongst you, an overnight camp site is desirable, but where this is not possible there is often a bunkhouse to provide economical accommodation, or, if all else fails, there's usually a farmer or landlord nearby willing to let you pitch a tent.

The 'mini treks' were designed round the idea of people travelling to the start of the walk on Friday evening, thus enabling a full day's walking to be achieved on Saturday. Sunday's mileage in most cases is rather less to allow the journey home to be accomplished comfortably that evening. It is possible to get to the start of each walk by public transport, although some services may be limited during the winter months.

A 'mini trek' weekend is also an ideal introduction for those of you thinking about attempting a long distance path. It acts as a taster for the longer routes and gives you the opportunity to test out your gear. For backpackers it's a chance to try out equipment and gauge just how much or little you can get away with. Weight, of course, is of paramount importance with every ounce (oops! gramme) counting, even to the extent of cutting down your toothbrush – yes, some of us actually do this! It's amazing how much you can reduce your overall weight by paying attention to these smaller details.

In conclusion then, a 'mini trek' weekend will hopefully be 'just what the doctor ordered'. So get out into the hills and blow those cobwebs away, but most of all enjoy yourselves.

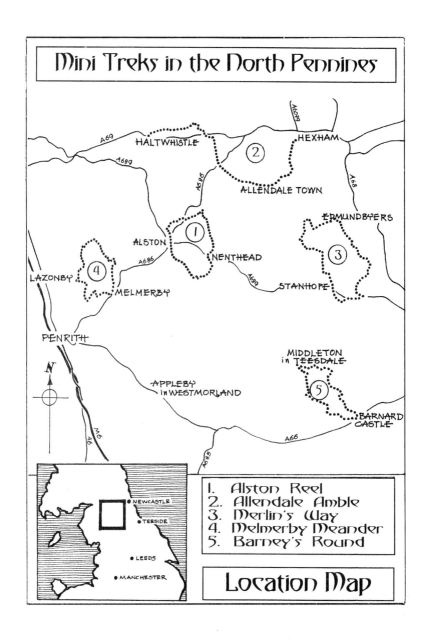

Mini Treks in the North Pennines

1. Alston Reel
2. Allendale Amble
3. Merlin's Way
4. Melmerby Meander
5. Barney's Round

Location Map

Introduction

Every walk has its own abiding memories but often one is more enduring than all the rest. My first view of High Cup Nick is just such a memory for me and will forever be associated with the Pennine Way which I walked some years ago. I can never forget the moment when we reached the rim of High Cup and first looked down. The sight beneath our feet of a horse-shoe of screes swooping down to meet High Cup Gill in the valley floor was absolutely stunning and I was filled with excitement and wonder. That was my first association with the delights of the North Pennines and I seemed to know at once that it would not be my last.

The North Pennines is a vast area which stretches from the A69 in the north to just below the A66 in the south; it is bounded by the River Eden in the west and the conurbations of Newcastle and Durham in the east. Designated an Area of Outstanding Natural Beauty (AONB) in 1988, it has been called the last great wilderness – a description it richly deserves, in my opinion. Its hills and dales are sparsely populated and there are vast tracts of moorland and bog without any habitation. This remoteness is one of the area's great appeals, and the fact that you can walk for miles without meeting a soul adds a unique sense of adventure to the walking.

The North Pennines span three counties: Northumberland, Durham and Cumbria, each with its own individual character. It contains seven major rivers whose dales together comprise the North Pennine Dales, an area as yet unspoilt by tourism and of exceptional beauty. Cross Fell, at 893 metres above sea level, is the loftiest summit in the North Pennines and is also the highest point for those travellers walking the Pennine Way which traverses it.

My interest in the area was rekindled whilst driving north along the A68 one day *en route* to Hexham. Away to my left stretched a tempting panorama of rolling hills and valleys and I was filled with a desire to see more. Unfortunately on that occasion I was unable to realise my wish but, several months later, one bright Saturday morning found me in Hexham market square, kitted out with boots and rucksack and ready for the off. I was rewarded that day with good weather and enjoyed an excellent walk which took me from the historic market town of Hexham, through Slaley Forest and up onto Blanchland Moor with its commanding views. The day culminated at the village of Blanchland which is surely one of the prettiest in Northumberland. Immediately I was hooked! I was to find on subsequent visits many such gems hidden away in this vast wilderness, all waiting to be discovered by the adventurous walker.

Being new to the area enabled me to see it with fresh eyes and the walking became a continuing voyage of discovery. I never ceased to be amazed at the grandeur of these wild and remote fells and the sharp contrast with the lushness of the valleys below. Water is a major feature, with the great rivers of the Tees, Tyne, Derwent and Wear all having their sources high up in the moorlands. (Incidentally, these moors are a renowned haven for wildlife; here the Hen Harriers breed, and Merlin and other rare species of birds can often be seen.) Lower down, powerful streams and waterfalls abound, their free source of energy having been harnessed over the centuries by the inhabitants of the North Pennines. In earlier times water was used to drive huge wheels for the grinding of corn and, later, to drive the machinery used in the lead mines. In the valleys, historic castles and abbeys stand as majestic reminders of the past. Another element of bygone times is the pele tower, built as a defence against the border raiders. These have been much altered through the intervening years but nevertheless are unmistakable, their battlemented towers standing out like beacons in the landscape.

While ancient settlers have made their mark on the landscape, the more recent workers in the old lead mines have left their own vast heritage behind. It's fascinating to discover traces of these mines and their associated industries, for they provide us with an insight into the lives of the people during this period. These remains have become softened with time now and blend almost imperceptibly into the landscape, so it's often difficult to believe that this was once the wealthiest lead mining area in Europe. (By the way, it's well worth remembering that all mine shafts are potentially dangerous and great care must be taken when approaching the old workings.) For more information about the lead mining industry a visit to the Killhope

Lead Mining Centre in Weardale is a must. Add to all this the legendary friendliness and hospitality of the local people and you have the perfect place through which to wander.

The walking of long distance paths is an ideal way to get to know and appreciate an area, but our busy lifestyles sometimes make it impossible to fit in these lengthy treks, occupying as they often do several days or even weeks. Frequently, however, a long weekend can be slotted into an otherwise hectic schedule. With this in mind I have devised a series of two-day 'mini treks' which offer an outstanding opportunity to become familiar with a part of our countryside. All of the walks can be reached by public transport which helps to ease the congestion on our already overcrowded roads. Although primarily devised as two-day walks, with a bus time-table and a bit of careful planning some could be split up into day walks if necessary. All are circular apart from the Allendale Amble, but even this should not be a problem as there is a regular bus and train service between Hexham at the finish and Haltwhistle at the beginning of the walk.

The Melmerby Meander is based in the Eden valley and as such may not be classed by some as truly part of the North Pennines. However, I make no apologies for including it, as this 'garden of Eden' with its idyllic red sandstone villages is dominated by the Pennine fells. The hamlets and villages at the foot of the Pennine escarpment and known as East Fellside, are situated in a truly Pennine environment. The people here are set apart from those who live in the villages along the banks of the Eden where the climate is kinder. Those who live on East Fellside have their lives shaped by the Pennine weather, their houses are built to withstand the notorious Helm Wind and their crops and cattle have to withstand a much harsher environment than those who live in the valley.

I have tried to ensure that there is a variety of accommodation at the overnight stages, but it has not always been possible to include a campsite in the planning. However, if you don't mind camping wild there should be no problem in the more remote areas, although you should always seek permission first. Alternatively, a request to the local farmer may prove beneficial, as I've discovered on more than one occasion.

As far as can be ascertained the routes follow rights of way, permissive paths, and in one or two places, *de facto* rights of way. Care must be taken during the shooting season which starts on the 'Glorious Twelfth' of August and continues through to 10 December. Access to some of the moors is actively discouraged at these times so it is particularly important that you check before setting out. This should not affect rights of way, however, but it is better to know whether a shoot is likely to be taking place, then you have the option of avoiding it, discretion being the better part of valour. The local Tourist Information Centre will either give you up-to-date information or failing that the 'phone number of the gamekeeper concerned. The above is pertinent to all the walks apart from Walk Four which doesn't include any open moorland.

The remoteness and ruggedness of the terrain in some parts means that adequate equipment is essential. Adverse weather conditions can be experienced at any time of the year – in the space of a few hours a storm can transform tiny streams into raging torrents, for example. Never cross rivers in these conditions unless you know what you are about, even if it means a lengthy detour. The ability to use a map and compass is essential, particularly as many of the paths are not yet waymarked or visible on the ground – although this position is gradually being rectified.

At the end of each walk is a space for your own personal log with just a few suggestions which the reader may fill in as desired. In compiling the list it occurred to me that some of your comments may be unprintable (possibly your comments regarding the author!) but then they're for your eyes only, after all.

The North Pennines area is easily accessible by road, via the M6 in the west and the A1 in the east. Perhaps more importantly, it can be reached by high speed rail links to Carlisle in the west and to Durham and Newcastle in the east. Extensive bus services link these mainline railway stations with the major towns in the area.

A visit to this unique area leaves the visitor with a lasting impression of broad panoramas and wild sweeping moorland interspersed with lush green valleys, each with its own magical river. I hope that you will enjoy discovering the North Pennines as much as I did or maybe you'll renew an old acquaintance – whichever is the case, happy walking.

Enjoy the countryside and respect its life and work.
Guard against all risk of fire.
Fasten all gates.
Keep dogs under proper control.
Keep to public paths across farmland.
Use gates and stiles to cross fences, hedges and walls.
Leave livestock, crops and machinery alone.
Take your litter home.
Help to keep all water clean.
Protect wildlife, plants and trees.
Take special care on country roads.
Make no unnecessary noise.
Remember it is an offence to dig up or pick wild flowers!

If you take only photographs and leave only footprints, you and those coming after you will be welcome.

WALK NUMBER ONE – CIRCULAR
'ALSTON REEL'
Alston – Nenthead – Alston

Total Distance 36.8 kms (23 miles)
Alston to Nenthead 21.6 kms (13.5 miles)
Nenthead to Alston 15.2 kms (9.5 miles)

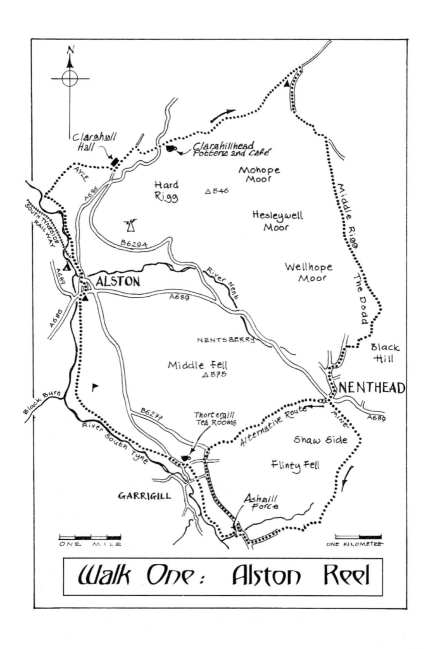

Walk One: Alston Reel

Walk 1

Day One
Alston to Nenthead

Distance 21.6 kms (13.5 miles)
Ordnance Survey Maps
1:25,000
    Pathfinder 559 – Slaggyford
    Pathfinder 569 – Alston
1:50,000
    Landranger 86 – Haltwhistle Bewcastle & Alston area.

*T*he day starts with easy walking through farmland before a climb up onto open moorland and the possibility of refreshment at the Pennine Pottery at Clargill Head House. An excellent track then takes you over Ouston Fell with its extensive views of the surrounding moors, before dropping down to West Allen Dale and Ninebanks Youth Hostel. The final stretch is a long gradual pull up Hard Rigg with superb views once more as you circumvent The Dodd. Then it's all downhill on track and minor road to reach the Quaker-built model village of Nenthead with its rich mining heritage.

Alston is situated on the confluence of the Rivers Nent and South Tyne and is surrounded by the highest fells in the Pennine Chain. It claims to be the highest market town in England but this is disputed periodically by Buxton at the southern end of the Pennines. An early settlement here grew enormously in the eighteenth and nineteenth centuries with the growth of the lead mining industry, when the town became a service centre for the mining communities, particularly at Nenthead and Garrigill. The steep, cobbled main street with its distinctive market cross, has changed little in the last 100 years and is a focal point for visitors from far and wide. Alston is a bustling town with a reputation for local specialities such as Cumberland mustard and Alston cheese. The town is officially in Cumbria although geographically and socially it is allied to Northumberland, a county which you will visit on today's walk. Northumberland is unique in being the only English county with its own tartan and its own musical instrument. The tartan has a history dating back to the fifteenth and sixteenth centuries, being originally woven from undyed wool of both black and white sheep in equal quantities. It is still worn today by Northumbrian pipers when attending official functions.

Leave the market square in Alston in a westerly direction, dropping down to the A686. Turn right here and follow the road, passing a garage on the left, before going over a road bridge. The river below is the Nent which has its source in the fells behind Killhope and Knoutberry hills. Just beyond here is a turning on the left signed to the South Tynedale Railway. Turn down here, go past the railway station, then left over the railway line and then immediately right in the car park. A footpath sign shows the way between a group of trees. When you emerge from the trees the River South Tyne is on

An old property in Alston.

your left and the railway line on your right, no chance of going wrong here!

The railway came to Alston in 1852 when the lead mining industry was going into steady decline. The line, which ran from Haltwhistle, closed in 1976 and the station now houses a cafe and the Tourist Information Centre. Fortunately, through the efforts of the South Tynedale Railway Preservation Society, trains run once again at Alston. At present both steam and diesel engines take visitors along part of the old route as far as Gilderdale but eventually an extension will be complete, taking the line even further to Kirkhaugh. Special theme trips are organised throughout the year including Santa Specials and a 'Roof of England' guided walks special. The sound of steam evokes happy childhood memories for many of us (I don't mind admitting my age), and excites even the youngsters of today.

Soon you reach a little gate, go through here and turn right on a narrow road, crossing over the railway line. After about 50 metres turn left onto a farm track signed to Paddy's Well Steps. Follow the track and keep straight on, passing a house on your left, until you reach a gate and stile in the dry stone wall ahead. Once through here keep on in the same direction until you reach a woodland. The viaduct may be glimpsed on your left through the trees, taking the railway over the river. As you approach the woodland your exit is over a stile in the wall on your right, a few yards from the field corner. Once over here climb up the hillside on the obvious path through the trees to reach a road at GR714482. Turn left here and follow this quiet country road for slightly under 800 metres (½ mile) to reach Randalholm Bridge.

As you approach the bridge you may be able to spot the site of Whitley Castle which is diagonally left on the fellside beneath Great Heaplaw. All that remains is a series of concentric grassy ramparts around a central platform. This was the only Roman fort constructed within the North Pennines and its purpose is uncertain. It was possibly built to exploit the lead mining in the area and supporting evidence for this are the lead seals from Alston, found at Stainmore, and Roman lead found at Corbridge, which contains a mineral wax found on Alston Moor. Whitley Castle stood on the line of the Maiden Way, a high level Roman Road which ran for 16 kilometres from the Roman Fort at Kirkby Thore in the Eden Valley, to Carvoran on Hadrian's

An aerial view of Whitley Castle *(David Shotter)*.

Wall. It was the second highest Roman road in Britain and was paved to a depth of one metre. How sad that today it is undetectable for much of its length – what a wonderful walk it would make.

Follow the road over Randalholm Bridge and then turn immediately right through a gate, signed to Ayle. After following the farm track for a few yards you leave it to strike uphill at a point where the track swings right. Walk uphill in a north-easterly direction towards the top corner of the field and the right-hand edge of Kirkside Wood. Go through the gate in the top corner where a backward glance will give you delightful views towards Alston. Follow the wheeled track to the far side of this next field where you reach a stile in the top corner. Keep straight across the next field and over a stile in the wall ahead of you. Keep the same direction in the next field until at the far end you see a gate in the wall on your right. Go through here and turn left along this narrow field to reach a further gate. Through here and follow the track towards a group of buildings. Go through a further gate and out onto the road. Turn right here and follow the road through the hamlet of Ayle. On the hill to the north of this tiny hamlet, is a working anthracite mine, the only one left in the area. The hamlet itself is like a relic from the past.

A view of Ayle village.

As you leave Ayle you pass a telephone box on your left followed by a farm on your right. Straight after this is a footpath sign on the right marked to Clarghyll Hall and a stile in the wall. Go over the stile and drop straight down through the field, to the left of a wooden fence and towards a shed in the far right corner of the field. Just to the left of the shed is a stile, take this and drop down left through this next field towards the far corner. Just short of the corner is a stile in the wall on your left, go over here and turn right, dropping down towards the Ayle Burn. Turn left just before a large ash tree to find a narrow path which takes you gradually down to the footbridge at the far side of the field. If conditions are slippery you may choose to keep to the high ground until you reach the far side of the field and then follow the dry stone wall down to the bridge.

At the far side of the footbridge go diagonally left uphill until you spot a dry stone wall at the top of the field and two prominent trees along it. You are aiming for the left side of the two trees where a stile should soon become obvious. Go over this stile, which is to the right of a gate, and head straight up the hill with a wall on your right and soon Clarghyll Hall will come into view ahead. Approximately halfway up this field is a line of trees, once through these you meet a track coming in from the right. Turn left along here and follow it towards the buildings of Clarghyll. Go through a gate across the track, which is waymarked, and follow the track between some old buildings. Notice the private chapel on your left. Follow the track up to meet a road at GR727493.

Clarghyll Hall is an example of an extended bastle and includes an impressive gable-topped tower. This is a later addition, created by a Victorian vicar in the 1860s and inspired by a visit he made to Germany. Bastle houses proliferate in the North Pennines and were frequently built by tenant farmers as a protection against cattle raiders. These thick-walled farmhouses had a basement which housed the animals and provisions. Entry was usually by a doorway in the gable end and ventilation consisted of two or three slit vents. Entry to the upper floor living quarters was by a doorway set in the south wall and accessible only by a movable ladder. In later years external stone stairs were added and there are many fine examples of this throughout the Pennines. One or two tiny windows provided light, with iron bars across the hole to prevent raiders from gaining access. Heat was provided by a fire set against one gable end, whilst the washing facilities consisted of a stone bowl set into the wall. The drain for this 'slopstone' ran out through the thick wall into a stone spout which ejected its contents onto the ground below. I'm saying nothing!

Turn left along the road and follow it past Clarghyll Colliery on the right. As the road swings left beside the colliery, keep straight on along a byroad following the sign to Leipsic & Long Cross. (You would be excused for thinking that perhaps you'd strayed into another country, particularly if you look further up the 1:50,000 map to see Moscow marked adjacent to Leipsic!) After approximately 400 metres (¼ mile) and just prior to reaching a gate across the track you'll see a sign off to your right to Ninebanks via Long Cross. Turn right here along a good track beside a dry stone wall, shortly to become a track between two walls. Follow this excellent track as it climbs steeply out of the valley and swings left to eventually reach the A686 at Clarghyllhead. Go straight over the main road and follow the metal track to reach the buildings at Clarghyllhead House and, with any luck, a welcome cup of coffee!

The Pennine Pottery is well worth a visit. The tea room and shop are converted from an old byre, with the tea rooms being the front two stalls. A wide variety of food is served with fresh bread baked on the premises. In good weather you can sit outside and enjoy the superb views across the valley to the moorland beyond. These are moments to treasure, to be stored in the memory banks for recall on dark winter days. The tea-room is open between April and the New Year but closed on Mondays.

After the pottery keep straight on along the track, through a gate across it and on towards the wood. A further gate takes you into the plantation, keep to the main track all the way through the plantation until you reach a gate which takes you out onto Ouston Fell. You have just crossed the boundary out of Cumbria and into Northumberland. Keep straight on following the wheeled track across the moor and after about 800 metres (½ mile) the track starts to drop down towards Sandy Ford at GR753505. A plank bridge here takes you over Sandyford Sike and the track, which is an old drove road, carries on at the other side. You are surrounded by bleak moorland all around you but there's security in the form of this excellent track which never falters on its way over the moor to West Allen Dale. The expanse of Whitfield Moor is over to your left and the pimple on the skyline is Pikerigg Currick.

It is worth pausing for a moment to drink in the atmosphere and experience the almost total silence, broken only occasionally by the familiar 'Go-back! Go-back!' call of the grouse. At moments like these you realise that the North Pennines justifiably lives up to its title of 'The Last Great Wilderness'.

As you start to drop down from the moor the West Allen Valley opens up before you with the unmistakable line of Middle Rigg in the foreground. This can be seen directly ahead of you above the dry stone wall and is your route out of the valley towards Nenthead. The track continues towards the wall and then swings left with it to reach a gate in front of some sheep pens. Make your way through the pens and carry on down the track which is between two walls and drops down all the way to a road.

The views are stunning as you descend steeply to the West Allen Dale. The hamlet of Ninebanks lies in the valley and just beyond is Monks Wood. This is a Site of Special Scientific Interest and extends to over 47 acres. It contains ancient oaks and many epiphytes: ferns, lichens and mosses which grow on organic debris on trees and branches and only thrive in a pollution-free atmosphere.

Eventually you reach the tarmac road at GR774518 where you turn right and follow the road for just over 400 metres (¼ mile) to reach Ninebanks Youth Hostel at Keirsleywell Row.

The building used to be a miner's cottage and the 'mine shop' of Keirsleywell Level. Mine shops housed the miners during the week; at the weekends they often had to walk many miles back home to their families. Conditions in the 'shops' were very basic indeed and overcrowding played a significant part in the spreading of infectious diseases. There's a poignant reconstruction of a mine shop at Killhope Lead Mining Centre at the head of Weardale.

In high summer the hedges bounding the road are full of wild roses which are a delight to the eye. These delicate flowers are followed in the autumn by bright red hips which shine like jewels amongst the thorny branches.

Keep on along the road to a fork, take the left one (passing Ivy Cottage on your left) and drop down to Park House amongst the trees. Keep

Ninebanks Youth Hostel

Appletree Shield Chapel.

straight on, passing the farmhouse on your left and going through a gate. Keep on the farm track until you reach a large barn on the left. Turn immediately left here before the barn, through a gate and across a yard and a further gate. Drop down through this field towards a building surrounded by trees in the far right corner of the field. Go through the gate in this corner and turn right onto a good farm track.

Soon you reach Nether House on your left and a telephone box outside it. Just after this, where the track swings away right is a stile in the corner. Go over here and drop downhill with a wall on your left to reach a footbridge. Once over the bridge follow the path round a ruined building and ignore the stile directly ahead of you but turn left going over a further footbridge at the confluence of the Mohope and Wellhope Burns.

The ruin is all that remains of Appletree Shield Chapel, one of the 'primitive' chapels to be found in the area. In the eighteenth century, with the rise in the North Pennine population due to the considerable growth of the lead industry, came the Methodist Revival. John Wesley was the chief evangelist for this movement and a tremendous traveller as well. On one trip he preached in Blanchland and Hindley Hill on the first day, rode to Nenthead to preach at 8.00 a.m. the following day, onto Alston at noon and then back to Hindley Hill in the evening. The third day he preached to a very large congregation in Allendale Town. He held great appeal for the miners as they were able to relate to a preacher who shared their own background. In contrast the wealth of the Church of England and its ministers only seemed to highlight their own poverty.

In the early nineteenth century the Primitive Methodist Connection was established. This break-away group (popularly known as 'Ranters') was in favour of great 'camp meetings', and popular tunes of the day were frequently incorporated into their hymns. Services were held in 'mine shops', barns and any other building available. When chapels were eventually built they were simple and functional and free of any architectural adornment. Later in the century this was all to change when Gothic architecture was incorporated into many of these chapels. The ruin here at Appletree Shield is a classic example of that early style. You need a vivid imagination to recreate the atmosphere of those early meetings, here in this lonely spot, but it's worth the effort. In inclement weather this is also a particularly handy place for a break.

After crossing the second footbridge, follow the path which makes its way up through the trees and go through the gate at the top and turn left, following the fence around the edge of the field towards Hesleywell Farm. Go through a gate in the top left corner of the field between two large barns. Go straight ahead across the farmyard to reach the road. Turn right on the road and almost immediately turn left over a stile in the wall, signed to Nether Harsley. Climb up through the field, keeping a short distance away from a wall on your right, aiming to the right of a ruined building which can be seen at the top. Some way to the right of this is a stile in the wall corner. Go over here (excellent views back over Ouston Fell which you crossed a while ago) and turn left along a walled track. Go through a gate which crosses this track and follow the track to a wall corner where the walls open out. Continue along the main track which soon splits, any track or path will do as they all meet up again in about 50 metres at a signpost situated close to a wall corner. To the left is a tarmac road going downhill through a gate – ignore this, turn right and follow the obvious track which swings round and follows a wall uphill.

Follow this good track with the wall on your left as it climbs steadily

A cairn on Middle Rigg

up onto Middle Rigg. Go through a gate on the track and keep on climbing (you've now left the wall on your left but there's one away to your right for guidance), until eventually the track swings away through a gate in the wall on your right about 700 metres (800 yards) from the previous gate. Do not follow the track through the gate but go left a few yards before it on a vague path which follows the wall on your right. Keep on, crossing over a track which comes in from the left across your path, until eventually you reach the corner of the dry stone wall on your right, approximately 800 metres (½ mile) away. The wall drops away right at this point at GR785476. Just before the wall corner the path enters a slight gully and you must follow this as it takes you away from the wall.

Ahead on the horizon can be seen the outline of The Dodd at 614 metres; just beneath this is a dark object which is in fact a cairn on Little Hill and your next objective. The gully can be a bit vague in places but persevere and keep aiming towards the cairn. (Carriers Hill is the raised area on your left whilst the ground drops away gradually on your right). Eventually you join a more defined gully coming in from the right and soon after a small cairn. Where the gully swings away left towards the tall cairn on Little Hill, another small cairn can be seen to the right of your path. Continue to follow the gully left when it all but disappears as you cross a boggy area. Make your way straight towards the cairn on the skyline.

On arriving, it's quite a surprise to discover that our cairn is only just over 2 metres high as it appears to be so much taller when you're walking towards it. From here, aim for a prominent finger post ahead on a compass bearing of 155°. This leads you to a track which takes you on the east side of The Dodd. At the finger post continue climbing towards the Dodd on a path which soon becomes a depression swinging round to the right. Shortly it joins a gully coming in from the right. Turn left here on a clear path (a pile of stones marks the spot) and 18 metres (20 yards) further on, a larger cairn confirms that you're on the right path. Follow the now obvious waymarked path in a southerly direction as you circumvent the summit of The Dodd.

This part of your journey coincides with the route of the Alternative Pennine Way, a 431-kilometre walk from Ashbourne in Derbyshire to Jedburgh in the Scottish Borders. It provides a superb alternative to the Pennine Way, avoiding most of the boggy sections of that famous long distance footpath. Dubbed 'The Gourmet's Pennine Way', the alternative seeks out suitable places for food and accommodation at the end of each day with often places to eat midday as well. What more could you ask for?

There are extensive views all around as you head towards the Cumbrian border. After a lot of climbing it's wonderful to realise that the route is now downhill all the way to Nenthead.

As you start to descend, ignore a track which branches off to the right uphill and keep straight on towards a dry stone wall ahead. Turn left on reaching the wall, following a wheeled track, until you reach a gate in the wall on your right. Go through the gate and enter

Looking down over Nenthead

Overwater near Nenthead

Cumbria at GR791452. Ignore the bridleway which is the obvious path going diagonally right and go diagonally left towards a broken-down wall. Make your way over the wall and turn right and follow it along – there is no path on the ground. Follow the wall to its far corner and then follow it left until you reach another corner and a wire fence ahead of you. The route lies over this wire fence but at present there is no stile to help you. The wall and fence are down in many places where other people have been trying to get over.

Make your way as best you can. Once over, turn right and drop down the hill with a wall on your right. From this viewpoint the houses of Wellgill can be seen in the distance on the outskirts of Nenthead. At the bottom of the field is a gate which takes you out onto a good track. Make your way over the gate and turn left along the track.

Follow this good track all the way down to Dykeheads and the road. Turn left along the road and follow it for 800 metres (½ mile) all the way down into Nenthead. Among the rough moorland pastures you can still see green fertile areas, some enclosing a ruined build-ing. These were the miners' smallholdings, provided by the London Lead Company as a form of land reclamation. Usually about 7 acres in size, these smallholdings enabled the miners and their families to rear animals for milk and meat and also to grow their own vegetables. When the mines closed, the land alone couldn't provide enough income and most families left the area. Many of these ruins are in magnificent locations with stunning views and would make wonderful homes – all you need is the lottery money!

Shortly before the road turns sharp right to drop down to Nenthead, you pass a group of houses on the right known as Whitehall. It was here that part of the mining workforce lived before the arrival of the Quaker Company. Eventually you reach the paved part of the road with its original surface of blocks or setts. On our right are some of the original 1825 model village miners' houses. Also on the right as you reach the main road stands the Methodist Chapel which was built in 1873 on the site of another chapel where John Wesley used to preach. On your left is an ornate cast iron fountain, similar to one in the centre of Middleton-in-Teesdale. Like the one in Middleton, it was erected by R. W. Bainbridge in 1877 on his retirement as super-intendent of the London Lead Company.

Nenthead is well provided with accommodation. There are two public houses, various B&B establishments and two bunkhouses. Provisions can be obtained at the village store, there's a cafe at the Nenthead Mines Visitor Centre and both the Miners Arms and the Crown Inn offer food and accommodation.

There is much to see at the Nenthead Mines Visitor Centre if you've the time to spare, including a new exhibition which tells the story of the mines, the village and its people. Nenthead is a model village built by the London Lead Company or the Quaker Company as it was more commonly known. The company transformed the area, building amongst other things a market-hall, school, chapel and a tall tower incorporating a clock known as 'Peter' which could be seen all over Nenthead. A public water supply was fitted in 1850, followed by a public baths and wash-house. The directors of the company were very aware of their responsibilities to their workers and introduced compulsory schooling for all children. This, along with a free reading room, built in 1833, was among the first to be introduced in England.

Beyond the entrance to the Nenthead Heritage Centre and over the bridge lies Overwater, a hamlet within Nenthead. Rising behind these houses is a steep valley known as Dowgang Hush. In the past, Dowgang Burn was repeatedly dammed higher up the fellside and the water suddenly released. The force of the water scoured away the surface soil, revealing the lead veins below. Hushing, as this method of prospecting was called, was used extensively in the North Pennines areas and the results are a distinctive feature in the landscape. The wooded valley around the burn became a local beauty spot and was used by miners and their families for a Sunday evening stroll after attending chapel. Nearby, Nent Force Level was a unique underground waterway, nearly three kilometres long, driven underground by a great engineer called John Smeaton. Started in 1775, it took 66 years to complete and its purpose was chiefly to drain water from the mines and to reveal new mineral veins. Part of it was navigable to boats, propelled along with sticks. Stories abound of Victorians holidaying in the area and taking boat trips along it. There is even a suggestion that one area was large enough for a dance floor and that it became know as Jennie's Dancing Loft! Nenthead, set high up in the rugged Pennine fells, is a fascinating place, rich in history from the lead mining era. It is reputedly the highest village in England (where have I heard that before?) with most certainly some of the highest churches and chapels.

Walk 1

Day Two
Nenthead to Alston

Distance 15.2 kms (9.5 miles)
Ordnance Survey Map
1:25,000
   Pathfinder 569 – Alston
1:50,000
   Landranger 86 – Haltwhistle, Bewcastle & Alston area.

---

*T*he walk starts with a gradual climb on an excellent track up onto the shoulder of Flinty Fell, passing through the remains of the once-flourishing lead mining industry. The air is sweet and the views superb as you drop down on the continuing track to reach the popular beauty spot of Ashgill Force. A delightful riverside walk follows to reach Thortergill and possibly a cup of tea. The final stretch is easy walking through fields and along riverside paths up the South Tyne Valley to reach journey's end at Alston.

Leave Nenthead by the fountain, crossing over the main A689 and keeping straight on towards Overwater. Soon you'll see a sign on the left for Nenthead Mines.

HERE A DECISION HAS TO BE MADE:

An excellent track starts here which will eventually take you all the way over Shaw Side and around Flinty Fell to reach Low Ashgill, a distance of some six kilometres (four miles). The public have enjoyed a *de facto* right of way on this track for many years, even though there is a short section approximately 600 yards long (on top of the

Smallcleugh Mine, Upper Nent Valley. *(North Pennines Heritage Trust)*

moor) which is not on the definitive map. I must stress that to the best of my knowledge no walker has ever been challenged when using the route. I have used it myself on many occasions along with hundreds of other people over the years. The track constitutes part of the Coast to Coast cycle route and is also part of another long distance walking route.

However, should any problem arise I am including here an alternative route which joins the original one at Ashgill Force. This route also provides an opportunity to shorten the day's walk by approximately 4.8 kilometres (3 miles) if this is needed, by leaving the B6277 (having crossed Alston Moor) and dropping down to the cafe at Thortergill where you can rejoin the original route. (This would be a great shame, though, as you'd miss out Ashgill Force, a major scenic attraction which is followed by a delightful stretch of riverside walking.) The choice is yours.

ALTERNATIVE ROUTE:

Keep straight on past the mine entrance and through the hamlet of Overwater, passing the Crown Inn on your right. Follow the road as it bends round to the right and then almost immediately left, away

from the river. The road climbs steeply and after a short distance
you reach a footpath sign on your right signed to White Sike Mine,
opposite to Bevan Terrace. Take the track to a gate which opens
onto the fellside. Continue along the obvious path as it goes uphill
and soon you join a broken down wall on your left. Follow this uphill
to reach a stile in the top corner of the field. Once over here keep
on in the same direction aiming to the right of an old barn. A marker
post can be seen on the skyline. A glance back will reveal a pleasing
picture of Nenthead in the valley below.

When you reach the marker post, just in front of the old barn,
keep straight on uphill, passing to the right of the barn. Carry on
uphill in the same general direction until eventually a conifer plantation
comes into view on the horizon. Keeping the same direction look out
for a marker post in a wall before the plantation. At the marker post
go over a stile in the wall here and follow the direction of the waymark
uphill again towards the trees. Go over two further stiles in a wall
and fence eventually to reach the plantation. Turn right here following
the waymarks.

Follow the path round the edge of the plantation before you start
climbing once more. Soon you reach a stile in the wall on your right,
go over here and follow the directional arrow diagonally right uphill
– a marker post can be seen on the skyline ahead of you. Go over
the stile adjacent to the marker post, and keep on along a vague path
in the same direction.

Ahead and over to your right can be seen an area of disused mines
and also Greengill Hush, both marked on the OS map. Soon you join
a wall running uphill on your right and after a short distance a stile
is reached. Go over here and turn immediately left following the wall
as it strides further up the fellside. Follow it over the watershed and
almost immediately a gate comes into view in the wall on the left.
Strike away from the wall here and aim diagonally right, cutting off
the corner and you'll see a marker post in the wall ahead of you. Go
over the stile here and keep on in the same direction following a
vague path towards a copse of conifers, the tops of which can be
seen in the distance (just to confuse things these are not marked on
my OS map). When you reach the trees turn right with them and
follow the edge of the wood to its extremity. At the corner of the
wood the trees enclosing Garrigill Burn come into view with the
B6277 in the foreground at GR750424. This is your destination. However the route turns left here with the wood, following it all the way
down to Garrigill Burn. When you reach a wall in front of the burn,

turn right with it and follow it until you locate a gap in the wall and a marker post. Go through here and drop down to the side of the burn and follow it downstream all the way to the road.

This little stretch of path makes for fascinating walking as the remnants of the old White Sike mine are all around you. Soon you pass a small quarry on your right where the miners quarried the stone to build all the mine buildings and bridges. Prior to reaching the road, an old mine entrance can be spotted on the other side of the burn and almost immediately after this you pass an old shaft alongside the path.

On reaching the B6277, * turn left and follow this road for just over 2.4 kilometres (1.5 miles) to the bridge at Ashgill Force at GR759405. Go over the road bridge and turn immediately right following a footpath sign to Ashgill. It is at this point that you meet up with the original route.

(* However if wishing to shorten the day turn left here along the road but only for a distance of ½ kilometre (500 yards). Then turn right at the crossroads until you reach the T junction at Thortergill at GR743420 where you rejoin the original route.)

ORIGINAL ROUTE:

Turn left at the entrance sign and go through the car park towards the mine centre. The car park stands on the former site of the mine washing floor. It was here that the rock was sorted before being sent to the smelt mills. Don't go into the centre but keep straight on along an excellent track which will eventually take you all the way over Shaw Side and around Flinty Fell to reach Low Ashgill, a distance of some six kilometres (four miles).

A short distance up the track you reach Mill Cottage Bunkhouse on the left and a gate across the track. (Mill Cottage was the original smelt mill manager's house.) Go through a kissing gate at the side of the gate and keep on uphill along the main track, ignoring all other tracks, as you pass through remnants of old mine buildings. There's a strong feeling of being thrown back to another age hereabouts, surrounded as you are by ruins of mine shops, mine openings, washing sheds etc. It doesn't take much imagination to picture a scene of intense activity with dozens of people working feverishly in amongst the spoil heaps. A note of caution, however – please don't enter any of the mine openings as this could be very dangerous! Also please don't pick up any rock specimens or wild flowers as this is a Site of Special Scientific Interest. The wild flowers found in the Upper Nent Valley are all lead-tolerant species and as such are unique.

After approximately 500 metres you reach a raised bank on your left and a red topped marker post, just before the main track swings right. If you scramble up the bank here you'll discover Handsome Mea reservoir. This was used as a collecting point for streams from all around the valley. Its water was vital to the mine and an aqueduct carried the water from the reservoir to power a waterwheel which was the second largest in the country. Now Handsome Mea is used by local outdoor pursuits centres for canoeing etc.

Continue on the main track, climbing all the way. There is running water all around you; burns pour down the hillsides to join the infant River Nent and the stone leats which carried water down to the dressing floor are also in evidence. Apart from water you may encounter cyclists coming down the track as this is part of the C to C route; this is the country's first National Cycle Route, stretching over 225 kilometres from the Irish Sea to the North Sea.

As you reach a ruined building on your left there are rewarding views back towards Nenthead and the Nent Valley. Eventually the

Handsome Mea Reservoir, up from Nenthead

Little Gill Ford

climbing is virtually over as you reach the watershed with moorland all around you. At GR784421 is a junction of paths; take the left one of these and after approximately 50 metres there's a track going off left towards Perry's Dam. Ignore this but keep on along the main track and very soon Ashgill Wood comes into view ahead in the distance; before this are the buildings of Priorsdale. Now the track starts to descend and you reach a gate across it. Once through here, continue to the buildings at Priorsdale where the track changes to a farm road. The estate here was owned by Hexham Priory in the thirteenth century and was later bought by the London Lead Company. It was their first purchase on Alston Moor and stretched from Nenthead to Garrigill. Go through a further gate at the entrance to Ashgill Wood and carry on down to the ford at Little Gill. Once you enter the pine forest the atmosphere changes dramatically, the bird song is muffled and there is an eerie quiet and stillness. After making your choice of ford or foot-bridge the road climbs uphill towards Little Gill Cottage, to flank Harelaw Hill.

When you reach the B6277 turn right for 300 metres towards Ashgill Bridge. Turn left immediately before the bridge at a footpath sign to Ashgill. The path follows a fence on your left initially as it drops down steeply. Ignore a path off to the right going towards huge boulders, unless you're a mountaineer, but keep straight on. Steps ease your passage at this point and then the main obvious path turns sharp right; follow it round and down towards Ashgill Force and the river. An incredible sight meets you as you start to descend and enter an amphitheatre of rocks – a torrent of water some 15 metres high surges dramatically over a rocky ledge, perfectly framed beneath the arch of Ashgill road bridge. Follow the path to the falls, taking care in wet weather of the slippery surface underfoot. Just before the falls and to your right is the entrance to Ashgill Horse Level. This old mine entrance, partially covered by a large boulder, was the start of the Wellhope Knot Vein which was worked in the 1820s and went as far as Ashgill farmhouse. The mineral from here made enough profit for the Quaker Company to buy the whole Ashgill estate. It is possible to walk behind the falls where legend has it that fairies used to dance wildly. You're quite welcome to join them but great care is needed in very wet weather.

The fairies weren't the only ones who enjoyed dancing – the miners were accomplished dancers themselves. They adapted the old tradition of sword dancing to their own needs, replacing the wooden sword with a rapper. This was a flat flexible steel blade with a wooden grip, normally used for cleaning the coats of pit ponies. Although the dance had to be adapted to suit the cramped spaces in the mines it apparently lost none of its vigour, speed and intricate steps.

When you're ready to leave, turn your back to the falls and follow the river downstream to the footbridge. On your left just before the bridge are some large stone bays or 'bouse toemes' used for storing the lead from the mine. Cross over the footbridge and follow the path beside the river as it rushes over a series of limestone falls on its way to meet the South Tyne River. Go through a kissing gate and walk on towards another footbridge. Do not cross the bridge though, instead go over the stile in front of you signed to Low Crossgill. In summer common spotted orchids and the rare white flower of the Parnassus Grass can be found at this spot. Follow the obvious path with the river on your left and at the end of the field leave the river briefly to reach a stile in the right hand corner. Once over here turn right back to the river again and a good path beside it. The river now enters a deep sided gorge which is very impressive, but take care if you decide to take a look as there's nothing to stop you plummeting to the bottom! There are many wild flowers along here and in autumn a host of wild fungi, including the edible boletus and the chanterelle. If you're knowledgeable about mushrooms you might find something for tea, or maybe you're like me, only comfortable with an expert beside you.

Follow this delightful path beside the river, passing a farm access bridge on your left. Keep on along the same side of the river until you reach Windshaw Bridge which is a stone single arched bridge at

GR749409. It's worth a look over the bridge to the gorge below which is seen here at its most impressive as the river carves its way between huge boulders. Don't cross the bridge though but go over the waymarked stile ahead and climb the hillside beneath the trees to reach a wire fence. You follow this left briefly, before climbing over a stile in it and carrying on uphill towards a stone barn in the wall on your left. The landscape opens out here and there are extensive views down the Tyne valley with Garrigill in the foreground. Go over a stile just before the barn and cross the next field keeping a short distance away from a wall on your right towards Pasture Houses.

View from Windshaw Bridge

If you glance over to the hillside on your left you will be able to see an excellent miners track winding its way downwards; this is the route taken by Pennine Way walkers as they make their way off Cross Fell which can be seen on the skyline. Cross Fell is, at 893 metres, the highest Pennine peak. I have my own memories of this track whilst on the Pennine Way some years ago. It comes at the end of a very long day from Dufton and just seems to go on and on. Fortunately for us there was a house in the valley bottom serving teas (sadly now gone); never did a drink taste so sweet – the nectar of the Gods! Many other people thought so too – the house was positively bursting at the seams and the poor woman was rushed off her feet. The track was used in the early twentieth century by excursion parties going to watch the sunrise from Cross Fell. They went by cart as far as the 'mine shop' (now a bothy known as Greg's Hut) and then walked the rest of the way.

At the end of this field go over the stile ahead, across a road and over a further stile ahead signed to Loaning Head and Garrigill. When you reach the farmhouse buildings go through the gate, and then diagonally left between buildings and left through a gateway. Turn immediately right behind a building and follow a wall on your right. Cross three fields in the same direction to reach the houses at Loaning Head. The path passes directly in front of some cottages before reaching a track. The cottages are former small holdings lived in by the miners' families.

The route goes right here, but if you wish to visit the pub at Garrigill you may turn left and follow the track downhill, over the river and into the village. It's then merely a case of following the road back over the river and turning left to follow the minor road for some 800 metres (½ mile) to rejoin the route at Thortergill at GR743420. The rest of us are off to an excellent tea-room at Thortergill so go right, up the cinder track for a few metres and when you reach a tarmac road turn left, following a sign to Force Green. Pass Loaning Head Farm on your left which contains a magnificent modern stained glass window.

Follow the track between buildings until you reach a gate and stile which takes you out into the fields once more. Spoil heaps can be seen uphill to your right.

Alston Moor is completely ringed with shafts going deep into the fellside. The early mines here contained a significant amount of silver in the lead which justified a Royal Mint in Carlisle to deal with the output, whilst the lead was used for roofing. Windsor Castle and Clairvaux Abbey in France both used Alston Moor lead.

Keep straight on with a dry stone wall on your left and, when the wall drops away left, keep ahead shortly to go through a gateway and on towards some farm buildings. At the end of the field go over a stile ahead and on to the ruined farm buildings at Dodbury. Make your way through the sheep pens and through a gate onto a good farm track between walls. Pass through another gate at the end of the track to come out onto a road. Turn left here and drop down on the road to reach the hamlet of Thortergill.

At the T-junction turn right and follow the road over a bridge to reach the tea-rooms and waterfall walk. This is well worth a visit with delicious homemade food in a beautiful garden setting and on the site of a former eighteenth-century mine. It is, unfortunately, closed on Mondays in the winter months. To reach the cafe, which is just out of sight round the corner, follow the gravel path beside the Garrigill

Burn. For a small fee you can take
the waterfall walk which winds its
way through a wooded gorge with
31-metre high cliffs for much of its
length. Whilst there keep a look out
for the ghost. 'The Lady' is supposed to be a grieving relative of
Thomas Little, a miner killed in the
Thortergill Low Level Mine in 1848
by a rockfall. There are some in the
village who will swear the Lady has
been seen quite recently!

Carry on along the road until you
reach a cemetery on the left. Just
prior to this on the left is a
large cigar-shaped mound covered
in trees. This is a waste heap from
the Thortergill Mine, which was
utilised as an embankment to carry
the railway. Immediately after the
cemetery is a gate and a sign to
Bleagate. Go through here and follow a path diagonally right to go
through a gateway at the bottom

Thortergill

far corner of the field. Keep straight on with a dry stone wall on your
right and ignore a track which drops down left to cross the river. Go
over a footbridge spanning a burn coming in from the right and follow
a wall on your left. Carry on in the same direction through fields and
a series of stiles passing Middle Craig Farm up the hill to your right.
There are some good examples of smoots along this section; these
are the gaps built low down in the dry stone walls for the sheep to
pass through whilst restricting the cattle. Keep straight on following
the waymarks all the way to Low Craig which is approximately 500
metres from Middle Craig.

When you reach the buildings follow the yellow marker post
directing you over yet another stile and follow the marks round to
the right of the farm buildings towards a gate. Go through a stile to
the left of the gate and follow the track towards a gateway, once
through here keep the same direction with a wall on your right to
reach another gateway. Go through here, past a ruined building on
your right. Here you must leave the track and go slightly left (it is

waymarked) immediately to the left of a section of dry stone wall. At the end of the field go over a double stone stile (there's a bit of variety for you!) and carry on in the same direction over a series of stiles eventually to reach the ruined buildings at Low Sillyhall (I couldn't believe the name when I first came across it on the OS map). There are tantalising views intermittently, between the trees on your left, down to the South River Tyne and away to the fells beyond. Follow the path to the left of the ruins of Low Sillyhall to reach a large fingerpost; you have now joined the Pennine Way which has come in from the left. Follow the obvious path beside a wall on your right, ignoring the first gap you come to and going through the next gap which is waymarked. Go slightly uphill towards a wall, over a stile, followed by a gate and on towards the buildings at Bleagate. There are magnificent views on your left of the Black Burn river coming in off the fells to join the South Tyne whilst to your right the TV mast is clearly visible on the top of Mount Hooley.

At Bleagate go through a small gate and drop down to the road. Turn left here towards the farm buildings. Go through the farm gate into a yard and over a stile to the left of a gate. Turn sharp right here, following a wall on your right. Keep the same direction through a series of fields, with the river away to your left, to Low Cowgap. These low-lying farms are some of the oldest in the area and many were at one time miners' smallholdings. Some have now found another use as holiday homes. On reaching a copse of pine trees, follow the waymark taking you left through a gap in the wall. Once you've passed the small copse of pine trees cross back through the ruined wall and carry on in the same direction as before and continue until you reach a footbridge taking you over Nattgrass Gill. In this next field and diagonally right uphill is Annat Walls which is clearly visible.

This was once a reasonable-sized hamlet frequently visited by the Border Reivers. A local author, William Wallace of the 1880s tells us that the families of old used to have axes and other weapons handy by their beds in case of these unwelcome visitors. The Border Reivers were a law unto themselves, plundering whenever and wherever they could, resulting in many houses becoming fortified as a means of defence.

Carry on in the same northerly direction through fields until eventually you reach a path beside a fence on your right. Negotiate another stile and follow a wall on your right with scrubland on your left. Cross over the remains of an old wall and keep right with a wall, avoiding a boggy area on your left to reach a gill coming in from the right and a stone step stile ahead. Keep straight on over the stile and along the edge of a line of trees, the path becomes elevated as you enter the woodland with a steep bank on your left. This is Firs Wood which was bought in 1946 for £100 and donated to the people of Alston by Mr K. A. Robson, Clerk to the Alston Rural District Council. It suffered badly from the Dutch elm disease but is gradually being restored. Red squirrels and the shy roe deer have been spotted in the wood and even on occasion the odd badger. Eventually the houses of Alston come into view. After passing a cemetery on your right you reach the Youth Hostel.

At the road, turn left and then left again to drop down to the main A686. Immediately before the main road, turn right up a set of steps towards the hospital. Follow this walled path until it comes out onto a road. Turn left here passing a school on your left to reach the Parish Church of Saint Augustine at the end of the road. A right turn will take you uphill to Alston market square.

Having completed the Alston Reel you may well wish to discover some of the delights of the town. The oldest part is the area known as the Butts which is directly behind the market cross. To wander up and down the twisting cobbled streets is to journey back into the past. Some of the houses here are so old that they need stilts to hold them up. Dating from the 1700s, one or two can still be seen with their original outside staircase leading to the first floor. The ground floor beneath was used to house the animals in the winter months which provided a useful heat source. Who needs central heating anyway! This area was once used for archery practice, which was compulsory for all men over the age of 16. An essential skill, much needed during the days of border strife.

The Parish Church of Saint Augustine, which you passed down the hill, is the fourth on the site. Inside is a fascinating seventeenth-century clock, once the property of the Earl of Derwentwater whose family dominated the area throughout the middle ages. Also on display is the foundation stone of the original market cross, erected by William Stephenson, a local lad who became Lord Mayor of London in 1764. The stone was removed from its original site at the market cross as it was constantly being damaged by runaway vehicles.

Alston's High Mill, lying behind the market cross in the Butts area, was established in the fourteenth century. Power for the mill came from a small mill race which flowed right through the town centre. The source of the water was a reservoir formed by damming the Overburn, a small stream at Fairhill, higher up the main street. The mill race also functioned as the town's main washing and sewerage system; ah! the joys of living in the 'good old days'. The course of it can still be followed today and a useful leaflet 'Water Power in Alston' published by the East Cumbria Countryside Project, will give you much more information. There are several places in the town where the mill race can be clearly heard beneath the flagstones. In 1767 the High Mill was designed and rebuilt by John Smeaton the famous engineer whom you may remember was instrumental in building the Nent Force Level underground canal. The mill was unusual in having a very narrow 25-centimetre wheel with a diameter of 9 metres. By 1817 the mill was in need of repair. Apart from other repairs the original wheel was replaced by a new 6.5 metre one with a much greater width of 66 centimetres. The main part of Smeaton's mill is still visible today, now owned by the North Pennine Heritage Trust. An exciting new project is in hand to restore the mill to its former glory.

Alston.

There are many pubs in Alston offering food and accommodation. Not quite so many though as in the late-nineteenth century when 24 are recorded for a population of 1370 inhabitants. Shops and cafes are plentiful, as are B&B establishments, and a camp site is situated behind the railway station.

Date Walked _____

Companions _____

_____

_____

Weather _____

Highlight of the Walk _____

_____

_____

_____

Any other memories _____

_____

_____

WALK NUMBER TWO – LINEAR
'ALLENDALE AMBLE'
Haltwhistle – Allendale Town – Hexham

Total Distance 45.6 kms (28.5 miles)
Haltwhistle to Allendale Town 26 kms (16.25 miles)
Allendale Town to Hexham 19.6 kms (12.25 miles)

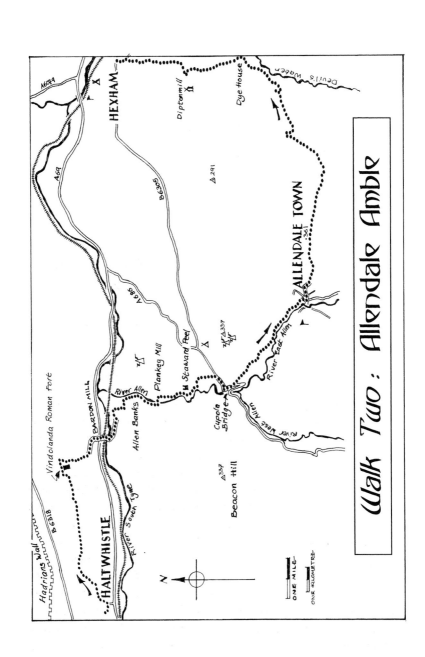

Walk Two: Allendale Amble

Walk 2

Day One
Haltwhistle to Allendale Town

Distance 26 kms (16.25 miles)
Ordnance Survey Map
1:25,000
    Pathfinder 546 – Haltwhistle & Gilsland
    Pathfinder 547 – Hexham & Haydon Bridge (tiny part)
    Pathfinder 560 – Allendale Town & Blanchland
1:50,000
    Landranger 87 – Hexham, Haltwhistle & surrounding
    area.

*T*his route is particularly full of interest with the initial climb
to High Plantation leading to our first sight of that majestic rock
formation the Whin Sill – hinting as it does of the presence of
Hadrian's Wall along its crest. Excellent level walking along the
ridge over Cranberry Brow soon follows, providing far-reaching
views on all sides before reaching the dramatic site of the Roman
fort at Vindolanda. A delightful walk amongst the trees beside
Chainley Burn then brings us down to Bardon Mill on the banks
of the South Tyne. There follows a walk through Allen Banks (a
sheer joy at any time of year), its excellent tracks enabling this
renowned beauty spot to be enjoyed to the full all the way to
Plankey Mill and beyond. A steep climb out of the Allen Gorge
brings you to the road above Cupola Bridge from where a series
of field paths carry you high above the East Allen River before
dropping down to the riverbank and the final few kilometres to
the remarkable Allendale Town.

   The walk starts in the market town of Haltwhistle (originally spelt 'Hautwessel' and still pronounced that way by some locals) which is known as the gateway to Hadrian's Wall. It is an ideal place from which to explore the spectacular remains of this extraordinary Roman memorial, designated a World Heritage Site in 1987. The town itself occupies a prominent position beside the great South Tyne River and is part of the English Border County of Northumberland, although it once claimed to be part of Scotland. It suffered during the border raids like many towns in the region; families on both sides of the borders fought endlessly for almost 400 years from the early fourteenth century and became known as the 'Border Reivers'. As a consequence, buildings in the area became heavily fortified and the remains of many of these are still in evidence. The Parish Church of the Holy Cross dates back in part to the thirteenth century and is one of Northumberland's finest. Much of the Early English church remains, including a nave with aisles. The effigy of a fourteenth-century knight and three ornately-carved coffin lids all date from this period. There is some beautiful stained glass, thought to be the work of William Morris, the famous Victorian designer of everything from stained glass to wallpapers. To the north of the town lies the

Haltwhistle

hauntingly beautiful Northumberland National Park while to the south is the equally beautiful North Pennines, itself an Area of Oustanding Natural Beauty.

Start from the market square in the centre of Haltwhistle GR 707641 where, embedded in the ground, is a huge rock extracted from the Whin Sill just north of the town.

This impressive monument was erected in 1994 as a symbol of Haltwhistle's links with the mining and quarrying industries and weighs 7 tonnes. This also marks the spot where a tree was set up twice a year during the annual fairs and decked with holly and ribbons. A bull was tethered and baited nearby and a good time was had by all (or nearly all – probably the bull was less amused). At the end of the fair the tree was sold and the resulting money spent in the ale houses.

Exit eastwards along Main Street, passing on your left the now deserted Red Lion Hotel.

The Red Lion's claim to fame is the relic of a pele tower which is incorporated into it, making it the oldest secular building in Haltwhistle. The walls of the tower at the east end of the building are over a metre thick. Extensive repairs and renovations are now going on within the building and all sorts of secrets are being revealed. An original seventeenth-century fireplace has been discovered amongst other things and finds include pottery and clay pipe fragments. The search is on for a secret tunnel, based on written sources and also local knowledge. When completed the Red Lion will be open once again as a hotel and possibly a guidebook will be available.

Carry on along the road, passing the Grey Bull on your left, soon to be followed by the Spotted Cow Inn on your right, as the road drops down towards the bridge over Haltwhistle Burn.

Take the first road left after crossing the burn, signed to Hadrian's Wall and follow it uphill until you reach a footpath on your right. This is situated immediately before the road swings away left and before Mount Pleasant House. Follow the path and steps behind the garden adjacent to the house – these lead you out into open fields. Go diagonally right up the hill towards a telegraph pole on the skyline. A backward glance shows extensive views of Haltwhistle and the fells beyond. On reaching the telegraph pole go through the kissing gate adjacent to it and into a further field. Cut diagonally left across the corner to reach a stile in the wall and curve diagonally right in the next field towards a dry stone wall. Follow the line of the wall until you reach a ladder stile on the right. Once over this, aim to the right of a building ahead and an adjacent large tree, behind which you'll find a ladder stile to take you onto a farm track. Turn right onto this and follow it towards a gate (do not go through this) but swing away left with the track until the wall on your right curves right. Go right with the wall and walk uphill on a good track towards a gate ahead in the dry stone wall.

Go through the gate and follow the obvious track, passing the building of Hollincrag on your right. The track winds upwards towards a plantation on the skyline and then curves left through a gateway in the wall. Keep straight on, going to the left of a pylon and following the path as it approaches a dry stone wall ahead of you. If you look diagonally left over the wall you will catch your first sight of the Whin Sill.

This is an amazing band of hard, crystalline rock which crops out in areas across Northumberland, the Pennines and Teesdale. These almost vertical crags create a spectacular landscape and are reminiscent of High Cup Nick, another dramatic manifestation of the Whin Sill in Teesdale. Hadrian was to make good use of this long line of crags when constructing the Roman Wall.

Follow the path right along the line of the wall until you reach a broad grassy track, turning left along this to reach a gate ahead of you. Once through here follow this track with a wall on your left; do not be tempted by the paths leading up into the crags – unless you have an alternative agenda – but keep to the main track as it curves away left and then right between some spoil heaps, to join a dry stone wall once more. Follow the path right along the wall side until you reach a minor road at GR 731656. Turn right here and follow the road for approximately 400 metres (¼ mile) to a point where it bends to the right. Go over a stile directly in front of you beside a gate, which leads onto an excellent track beside a wall which runs straight for just over 2 kilometres.

The raised ground over to your left is the course of the old Roman Road, known as Stanegate, which was the main cross-country link between the forts of Carlisle and Corbridge and predates the Roman Wall. North of Stanegate lies the Vallum which runs more or less parallel to the Wall and was a defensive ditch approximately 3 metres deep. North of the Vallum at a distance of usually 63 metres runs the Wall itself, taking advantage of the high crags of the Whin Sill. Even further north was another defensive ditch, built to protect the northern side of the Wall – the Romans weren't taking any chances!

Hadrian's Wall itself stretches some 46 kilometres from the Solway Firth on the west coast to the mouth of the Tyne in the east. It was a remarkable feat of engineering, but much of it has disappeared in the intervening centuries. The finest part is the 6-kilometre stretch here along the crags of the Whin Sill where there are still many impressive and near-complete remains to be seen. Away to your right are superb vistas encompassing the South Tyne valley and beyond onto Plenmeller and Ridley Commons.

As you approach the farm buildings of Cranberry Brow, Whinshields Crags come into view away to the left, along the line of Hadrian's Wall and on the route of the Pennine Way. This is the highest point of the entire wall at 345 metres above sea level. At the farm the path changes to tarmac for the last stretch before reaching a minor road. Turn left here and then almost immediately right on a track which takes you to the buildings at Layside. Follow the track round to the left of the farm buildings and out through a gate at the far side. Cross

Whin Sill from Crowberry Farm.

the field diagonally right to a corner, where a ladder stile will take you into a further field. Keep straight on with a fence on your right until you drop down to Bean Burn hidden among the trees.

This is a delightful little spot which is carpeted with cowslips in early summer. Once out in the fields again walk towards a stone building and pass to the right of it. This area is know as Kit's Shield, the word 'shield' being derived from the Norse 'shieling' or 'summer hill pastures'. Many shielings would only be occupied in the summer months by shepherds and herders when the sheep and cattle were driven to the upland pastures.

Keeping in the same direction, walk towards a band of larger trees where you meet a stile to the left of an old holly tree. Once over it keep on in the same direction (i.e. easterly) across some rough grass towards a gate. Turn left through the gate and follow the track through a further gate where one of the reconstructions on the site of Vindolanda comes into view to the right. Follow the track all the way to the road and turn right to reach the Roman fort of Vindolanda.

Vindolanda has a long and complicated history, with the earliest Roman Fort on the site, built of earth and timber, predating Hadrian's

The Roman Fort of Vindolanda. (*David Shotter*)

The Roman temple at Vindolanda.

Wall by more than 40 years. The headquarters building is very well preserved whilst west of the fort a civilian settlement has been uncovered. These excavations have resulted in a fascinating insight into the way of life of the families of the legionaries. Vindolanda was a main garrison fort and was home for up to 500 Roman auxiliary soldiers. Reconstructions of the Wall and one of its towers are of particular interest whilst the museum, set in ornamental gardens, is host to many unusual and well preserved artefacts from the Roman World. If you have plenty of time to spare it is well worth a visit; however, there are still many kilometres to go and more splendid things to see.

Carry on along the track which skirts the Roman Fort and very shortly you reach a gateway on the right giving a clear sight of part of the excavations. Eventually the track drops down to Codley Gate Farm. Look through the gate on your left, directly opposite the entrance to the farm, and you will see 'Chesterholm Roman Milestone'. This stands where the line of the Stanegate crosses the Chainley Burn. Now keep straight on up the road to a path on your right signed to Bardon Mill. The entrance to the path is flanked by two white lions and is also the entrance to Vindolanda Museum which is housed in a country house known as Chesterholm. Follow the waymarks directing you left when the track forks just before the museum and then almost immediately right at another fork in the track to drop down through the trees.

You emerge as onto a stage setting framed by trees and with a Roman temple laid out before you reflected in the water which gently cascades through a beautiful and ornate garden! This delightful scene is part of Vindolanda and fortunately for the walker the public footpath runs alongside, allowing us all to enjoy this little glimpse of Arcadia.

Follow the well marked path over the burn and then alongside it. Eventually the path leaves the water-side and takes you over a stile. It climbs initially in line with the burn, before levelling off and eventually reaching an isolated building at Low Fogrigg. An obvious track takes you on to a gate and once through here follow the track with a woodland on your left to a further gate. At this point walk diagonally right across the field to the right of a large pylon to reach a gate at the far corner which takes you out onto the road at which you turn left. At the road junction turn right, signed to Bardon Mill, and follow the road as it bends right past Cragside and drops down towards the A69.

Just before reaching the main road, approximately 90 metres (100 yards) short of it, you reach a track off to your left which is metalled as far as a gate. Follow this track (it runs parallel to the main road but makes for much pleasanter walking) until it approaches a gate leading to a private house. Veer away right here to a gate in the wall corner which leads you out into fields. Keep to the wall on your left and go through a further gate and drop down left to the A69. Cross with great care and take the track directly opposite, down to Bardon Mill. The track brings you out in the middle of a large pottery adjacent to the Bowes Hotel.

The pottery was originally a woollen mill before becoming a works for the making of drainage pipes. Fireclay for their manufacture was taken from an adit adjacent to Chainley Burn which you have just been following; no doubt the mysterious concrete blocks we have encountered were involved in the process somehow. The original chimney and kilns can still be seen at the bottom of the hill which you have just descended. The more recent kiln, adjacent to the road, was constructed when the owners made the changeover to making decorative ceramics which had become necessary with the advent of plastic pipes.

If you're in need of refreshments the Bowes Hotel may be open and there is also a village shop across the road. Unfortunately this is the only place where you can purchase anything for the rest of the day so make sure you're well stocked up!

At the road take the track directly opposite signed to the station and then turn left and walk along the station platform. Keep on at the end of the platform, following the fenced path beside the railway line to reach a road. Turn right here and cross the railway line, taking particular note of the notices relating to the red and green lights. Follow the track down to the river and over the bridge. Turn left along the lane and follow it as it leads the way to the delightful hamlet of Beltingham.

On your left we pass the Beltingham Nature Reserve which is home to many wild plants and is designated a SSSI (Site of Special Scientific Interest). The ground hereabouts is grassland contaminated with heavy metal. Lead and zinc, resulting from the mining activities higher up

The chimney at Bardon Mill.   A kiln at the pottery at Bardon Mill.

Beltingham.

the fellsides, has been washed down to produce a unique soil structure which has had the happy result of sustaining some rather special plants.

Beltingham occupies an idyllic spot in the Tyne Valley, the occupants of its charming homes seeming to exist in an otherworldly atmosphere of peace and quiet denied to most of us. On the inside of the distinctive lych gate leading to the church and adjacent to the seat is a plaque commemorating the fact that the gate and extension to the church yard were presented in 1904 by Francis Bowes-Lyon, an uncle of the Queen Mother. (The extension forms the final resting place of a number of members of the Bowes-Lyon family.) A further connection with the Queen Mother can be seen in the form of a cherry tree planted by Her Majesty in 1989 a little distance to the right of the path leading to the church door. The churchyard also contains a number of historic yew trees, thought to be the oldest in the country. The one on the north side behind the church is reputed to be over 900 years old and although hollow it is still growing vigorously, its ancient trunk clamped by iron bands. Yew trees were planted for several reasons, one of them being to protect the church from the elements, to ward off evil spirits and (being so long-lived as to be almost everlasting) were seen as appropriate symbols of the

Christian vision of eternal life. On a more practical level, the wood was often utilised for making longbows and so played a major role in the defence of the realm.

The church contains a 'leper squint' in the north wall of the chancel. These slits in the wall were so named because they enabled members of the congregation excluded from the service for any reason (such as infectious diseases) to see the altar. As there was a leper hospital nearby this seems feasible. However, due to the angle at which the squint is set, there is a theory that a priest's cell once existed where the present vestry stands. This would enable the occupant to watch the service but also to guard any ornaments placed on the altar.

The Martyr Bishop Nicholas Ridley was baptised at Beltingham Church and his memory lingers on in the parish. He led an apparently blameless life, becoming Bishop of Rochester in 1547 and then Bishop of London in 1550. However, he was committed to the Tower in 1553 after writing a treatise on Transubstantiation and was burnt at the stake opposite Balliol College, Oxford on 16 October 1555. An impressive monument marks the spot to this day.

After passing the church and a cottage, turn left at a wide grassy area, signed to Allen Banks (notice the Victorian post box set in the wall on your right). As you pass a walled garden on your left look out for a knight in shining armour flanked by a hedgehog, a tortoise and two eagles (the word 'wall' is the clue). Drop down to a little burn and follow it left. The path crosses it before climbing up out of the trees to open fields. Keep straight on, following a hedge on your right to reach the road at Ridley Hill GR793640. Turn right here and follow the road through the picturesque hamlet of Ridley

After a twist in the road and at the end of a mature plantation on your left a wide track off to the left is reached. Take this, following a fence on your right and passing to the right of a grassy knoll to reach a dry stone wall, again on the right.

This is in actual fact a ha-ha belonging to Ridley Hall which eventually comes into view over to the left. (The ha-ha was thought to have been introduced into England by the landscape gardener Charles Bridgeman and constitutes a sunken fence or wall bounding a park or garden. It needed to be deep and wide enough to prevent cattle from crossing into the garden but had to appear invisible from the house to create the illusion of the garden and surrounding countryside merging imperceptibly together. The name comes from the obvious cry of surprise issuing from the unwary at discovering the obstacle.) There is no access to the hall itself but a car park and picnic area enable the public to gain access to Allen Banks which you are approaching. This is all owned by the National Trust and was a gift from the Honourable Francis Bowes-Lyon.

At the end of the ha-ha we reach Allen Banks which consists of 200 magnificent acres of hill and river, with numerous waymarked woodland and riverside walks crisscrossing its dramatic scenery. Turn right on a good track to reach a fork after a few yards at which we go left.

There is superb walking along here with the ground dropping away steeply on your left down to the River Allen, where a suspension bridge can soon be seen in the bottom of the gorge giving access to a footpath on the other bank. Allen Banks contains an incredible variety of trees which are a picture at any time but particularly in their autumn glory. Many of their trunks are covered in various different lichens which make patterns reminiscent of abstract paintings whilst emerald green mosses cling to the rocks higher up the gorge.

The path drops down through the gorge to a bend in the river at a spot where several large trees have been felled. This open area, backed by Raven Crag, gives you the opportunity to take in the scale of this deep-sided gorge.

The water is deep enough to swim in and with its accompanying pebbly beach makes a very pleasant spot for a break if time permits. There is a fantastic array of twisted tree roots here where the sandy soil has been washed away by the action of the river, making intricate natural sculptures on the river bank. The path leads on beside the river eventually to reach Briarwood Nature Reserve, an ancient woodland with heavy metal-contaminated grassland as at Beltingham Nature Reserve. The small ruined building on your left which supports the Nature Reserve sign is thought to be associated with the lead mining industry and was possibly used for smelting. The woodland hereabouts is home to many wild flowers and wild life including roe deer and red squirrels. After approximately 90 metres (100 yards) past the ruin, at a fork in the path, go left over a foot-bridge and up the steps cut into the slope ahead of you. Keep on the main path over the slope to drop down to the suspension bridge at Plankey Mill.

My own thoughts on first reaching this spot are unprintable as I was expecting a foot-bridge and have a dread of suspension bridges. My walking partner at the time shared that same irrational but nevertheless very real fear. However, the alternative was a long detour and a change in my planned route which I had no desire to make so, taking a deep breath, we edged our way across. Thank goodness there was no-one else around to watch the spectacle.

Turn right on the far side of the bridge and follow the river bank on its eastern side. Here at Plankey Mill the land opens out a little and forms a popular and attractive camping spot in summer. At the end of the field the path curves left to a waymarked gate and stile where a National Trust sign proclaims 'Staward Gorge'. Follow the forest track right for approximately 360 metres (400 yards) where another path forks away right. It's worth sparing a couple of minutes here to find some wooden steps which take you down through the trees to a little beachy area backed by a rocky escarpment.

Here is a rather strange phenomenon because, when examined closely, the water appears to flow uphill. (No, I hadn't just emerged from

The suspension bridge at Plankey Mill.

An optical illusion at Staward Gorge – the water appears to be flowing upwards!

the local hostelry!) It's an optical illusion of course, but fascinating nevertheless.

> Otherwise carry on uphill on the forest track towards the high ground on which stands the remains of Staward Pele. Cross over a footbridge and at a fork in the path follow the left hand one uphill. After a few yards at the next fork in the path turn left again and climb steeply to reach the ruins of Staward Pele.

This medieval building was once a strong defensive site positioned as it is, high on a spur of rock. It was held by the Friars of Hexham until the fourteenth century before subsequently changing hands many times. There are records indicating that there was a portcullis and a drawbridge, though it's hard to imagine these things now.

> Do take great care around the ruins as the ground drops precipitously away through the trees. After leaving the Pele keep straight on along the ridge to reach a further ruin on your left which was the gatehouse. The site is owned by the National Trust and is designated an Ancient Monument.
> A few yards further on are viewpoints from the nearby crags on

either side of you. These offer stunning views on both sides: on the right, the River Allen can be seen running through the heavily wooded gorge while distant moorland overtops the scene – to the left you can gaze down towards the Tyne Valley and Haydon Bridge, backed by the line of Hadrian's Wall. I'm sure you don't need me to advise you that one false move here and the Mountain Rescue would have to pick up the pieces! Carry on along the wooded ridge which, because of its lofty position, gives you the feeling of walking on air. As you approach the end of the ridge you reach a fork in the path – turn left here towards a gate and stile ahead. Once through here you are out in open fields and can see your next destination, the ruins of Gingle Pot, diagonally right of you on the horizon. Follow the broad grassy path directly ahead of you as it contours the ridge above Staward Pele Wood on your right, eventually to reach the ruins.

Pass through a gate and follow the track (alongside a dry stone wall initially) and soon you reach the A686 road. Turn right along here and take care as it can be a busy road. Follow it for just over a kilometre (¾ mile), there's a grass verge for part of the way, as it zig-zags in hairpin fashion down towards Cupola Bridge. As you approach your turning-off point, occasional glimpses of a road may be encountered down the steep embankment to your right.

This road goes over Cupola Bridge, upstream of which is the meeting point of the East and West Allen rivers. The open ground near the bridge is the site of a large smelting mill which ceased operating in 1816. A low-arched furnace used in the smelting process was called a 'cupola' furnace, hence the name of the bridge.

At GR802589 is a broad track going up diagonally left off the road at a point approximately 45 metres (50 yards) before a bend in the road and a 'SLOW' sign painted on the tarmac. A footpath sign marks the spot. Follow this track beneath the trees to reach the open fields. Pass through a gate and follow the path alongside a dry stone wall with excellent views visible above the top of it. (A backward glance over this wall shows the meeting point of the rivers East and West Allen mentioned earlier.) Go through a gate ahead marked with a directional arrow and in the next field follow the path as it gradually curves uphill to meet the old railway track in the far corner of the field.

Cross over the railway track and a stile and carry on into the next field, climbing uphill towards Bishopside, following a fence on your right. Turn right at the end of the fence to reach a gate and the buildings of Bishopside. Once through the gate turn right between the farm buildings. Follow the obvious track across the fields to the next group of buildings, turn left at the road and then almost immediately right, indicated by a footpath sign. Cross the next two fields in the same direction and then in the third one cross diagonally left to reach a gate in the far corner of the field. Once through the gate, walk diagonally left again towards the farm buildings ahead. Cross over the stone stile beside a gate and keep straight on adjacent to a wall on your left with a mound on your right. Then follow the wall as it swings away left to reach a further stone stile ahead. Once over, turn immediately right and follow the wall and fence. As you walk down this field Allendale Town comes into view directly ahead of you in the distance above a group of trees. At last the day's end is in sight and there remains only 4 kilometres of easy walking to reach it. In the following field keep the same direction and where the wall veers away right, walk diagonally left to a gate which leads out onto the farm road.

Turn left and then right following a sign to Allenmill Bridge. Follow

Blackett's Level

this good track as it curves left and on reaching a gate turn immediately right in front of it, over a stile and down a hill. Directional arrows point the way downhill on a broad grassy path, curving right towards Owlet Hall. Pass through the gate to get onto the railway track and then turn immediately left through another gateway. Keeping a short distance away from the fence on your right, walk towards a lone tree which bears a waymark. Turn left on reaching the tree and go across the field to a ladder stile in the wall ahead. (This may seem unnecessarily tortuous but a look at the 1:25,000 map will show you the line of an old wall the top of which you have just walked along.). Once over the stile, turn right and head for a further stile on the edge of a belt of trees.

Follow the path down to the River East Allen, which is rather steep in places. Once at the bottom follow the obvious path as it wends its way beside the river all the way to Allendale Town. This makes for very pleasant walking with wild flowers in summer along the water's edge, amongst them the very pretty Mimulus or monkey flower which is a garden escapee found mostly by streams or rivers. Eventually you reach a foot-bridge known as Jeff's Bridge which takes you over a burn. Cross over and have a look round to the right where you will see a plaque on the bridge which states, 'In commemoration of W. J. Carruthers, farmer of Lead Hall, Catton 1911 to 1994'. After just over a kilometre (¾ mile) the B6295 and Allen Mill Bridge are reached. The area across the bridge here was the site of an old smelt mill which was in use for two centuries before closing in 1897. Cross over the road and carry on alongside the river, following a sign to Allendale Town and ignoring any footpath off to the left. After crossing another footbridge you reach the ruins of an old winding house and the sealed-off opening to Blackett Level.

This is an old mine opening which was planned to run for 4.3 kilometres to Allenheads but was finally abandoned after only 3 kilometres. Its purpose was to act as a drainage system for water from the mines and also as a possible new source of lead ore.

Soon the path leaves the river bank and climbs uphill towards the town. On reaching the road turn left along 'The Peth' and upwards into Allendale Town.

There is every amenity in the town including many pubs and cafes where you may slake your thirst. For a list of B&Bs see Additional Information at the back of the book. There's no official camp site

Allendale Church sundial

but an enquiry at one or two of the local pubs is likely to yield the name of a local farmer nearby willing to help.

Allendale Town is a delightful Northumberland market town and was once the centre of a thriving mining community. Lead mining in Northumberland began in Roman times and continued, apart from the period of the Dark Ages, until the 1920s. The town stands 431 metres above sea level and claims to be the geographical centre of Great Britain. To further its claim there is a sundial on the church recording its latitude of 54° 50′ which is reputedly half-way along a line running from Beachy Head on the south coast of England to Cape Wrath in the north of Scotland. Believe it or not, the challenger for this position is the town of Hexham, our destination tomorrow. Which one is the true centre? Your guess is as good as mine; having measured the aforementioned line, neither seem to do any more than form a rough approximation to half-way. Hexham doesn't appear to be on the line at all! Perhaps it depends on which projection your map uses so, considering the lack of hard evidence, judgement has to be reserved.

The church itself has a carved lych gate which stands as a memorial to the two World Wars and was erected in 1920. Inside the church is a rather wonderful reredos of alabaster which incorporates a mosaic depicting the Last Supper. The town was the centre for the agricultural hirings, held twice a year, when labour was bought and sold. These were accompanied by a fair and were occasions of great merriment with much music and dancing when no doubt the Northumbrian pipes would be in great evidence. These are played under the arm like the Irish pipes and are largely unknown elsewhere.

Allendale's main claim to fame today is its spectacular Fire Festival which is held each New Year's Eve. Its origin is unknown but this mid-winter celebration of light and life has been going on since Celtic times. At approximately 30 minutes to midnight, men dressed in outlandish costumes and known as 'guisers' enter the market square from the direction of the church, bearing on their heads huge barrels of blazing tar! The procession eventually makes its way to the centre of the square where a huge bonfire stands. Each in turn tips his flaming barrel onto the bonfire and, as the clock strikes midnight, the whole conflagration erupts to send flames shooting high up into the night sky.

Allendale fire festival

Walk 2

Day Two
Allendale Town to Hexham

Distance 19.6 kms (12.25 miles)
Ordnance Survey Maps:
1:25,000
    Pathfinder 547 – Hexham & Haydon Bridge
    Pathfinder 560 – Allendale Town & Blanchland
1:50,000
    Landranger 87 – Hexham, Haltwhistle & surrounding
    area.

*T*oday's walk begins with a steep climb up onto windswept moorland which is spectacularly covered with purple heather in late summer. On the moors the walking is easy and relaxed, enabling the superb views visible on every hand to be enjoyed to the full. From Burntridge Moor the route makes a leisurely descent through rolling farmland and lush pastures to the picturesque Dye House. Further undulations lead on to more scenic delights at Diptonmill before an ascent to the dizzy heights of 211 metres prefaces a final drop down to the fascinating and historic market town of Hexham.

Leave Allendale market place on the B6303 towards Catton and turn right up Shilburn Road which is directly in front of the Board School. Pass the Fire Station on your left and go through the hamlet of Shilburn. The road, which is very quiet, leads only onto the moor and provides the opportunity to take in the extensive views which progressively unfold as you climb higher. After just under 2 kilometres the tarmac swings right to Glen Hill Farm but continue straight on to the open moor to follow the obvious track, signed to Hexhamshire.

Allendale Town.

In springtime this area is home to many nesting birds and therefore it's important that you take note of the cautionary notice to this effect as you enter the moor and keep to the track. If you pause for a moment you may be fortunate to hear their calls all around you as I did one spring day.

In late summer the moors around you are ablaze with purple heather stretching as far as the eye can see. Such heather moors are a feature of Northumberland and are a result of forest clearance which, followed by heavy rainfall over a period of many years, turned the high ground into blanket bog. Sheep grazing and rotation burning keep the heather in perfect condition for the rearing of grouse. Grouse shooting provides work for many in the local community and the shoots begin on 12 August (walkers take note).

Soon you reach Long Rigg and a bridleway sign. This is the highest point of the day's walk and there are panoramic views to be enjoyed from here – ahead into Hexhamshire and behind into Allendale, while over to the left Hadrian's Wall greets us once more. From here, follow the marker posts until the far side of the moor is reached at a junction of paths at GR881554 which is well signed. Over to your right is a long ridge known as Broad Way which culminates in the peak of King's Law almost opposite you. Broad Way was an old carrier's way used for transporting lead ore, food and other commodities to and from the remote lead mining areas. A marker post at this spot indicates the way to Kingslaw Plantation; follow its direction straight on through a gate ahead from where you drop down to reach a road. Turn left and follow the road for approximately 800 metres (½ mile) to GR892550, at a point about 90 metres (100 yards) before the road bends away left. (You will have passed a track coming in on both sides of the road just prior to this but unfortunately neither are rights of way.) Pass through the waymarked gate on your left and drop down left to reach a broad track called the Dragg. (This is a Permissive Path which could be closed at some future date. If this is the case there is an alternative.)

ALTERNATIVE: Carry on along the road all the way to Kingslaw Plantation, which you reach after a sharp bend in the road. You'll see a stile in the wall on your left. Go over here and follow a wall on your right. Soon the farm of Gair Shield comes into view over the wall and the ground drops away left towards Rowley Burn. Just before the end of the field you reach a gate in the wall, pass through here and turn immediately left to follow the wall once more. Go over the stile in the far left corner of this next field, turn left and follow the wall to a gate. Once through the gate turn right and follow a fence, passing to the right of a copse of trees to reach Rowley Head Farm at GR 907561. Follow the track through the farm buildings, exiting right-handed once you've passed the farm house, on a good track towards a plantation. Shortly after the track swings left you will see a gate and stile on your right and this is where the other route joins you.

OTHERWISE turn right along the track and follow it all the way to the road at GR904567. This level track was constructed earlier this century when the valley was used for forestry and the track helped in the extraction of timber needed as fuel for the smelt mills. This is excellent walking along here with increasingly dramatic glimpses down through the trees of Rowley Burn. As you reach Goats Crags the sides of the ravine become precipitous and the trees appear to be clinging on for dear life. On reaching the road, turn right for approximately 90 metres (100 yards) and go through a gateway on your right which is waymarked. Follow this farm road all the way up towards Rowley Head Farm. As you reach the brow of the hill you will see a gate and stile on your left which are again waymarked. (ALTERNATIVE ROUTE JOINS HERE). Go through here and follow a fence on your right, heading towards Hexham. Go over a further stile adjacent to the plantation and at the end of the field through a further gate. Once through this follow the directional arrows diagonally left across the field to a stile in the far corner. Keep the fence on your left in the next field to reach Salmon Field Farm and a tarmac road.

Cross over the tarmac and go through the gate ahead. Keep a fence on your right and cross two fields, walking towards a plantation. In the third field go through a gate on your right and follow a fence on your left up the field to a gate which leads onto a green lane. This leads to Aydon Shields Farm. On reaching the tarmac, turn left to go through the farm buildings and pass to the right of a big barn (the farm house is on your right). Go through a gateway and turn right immediately to go diagonally across a patch of ground to reach a gate in the corner. Once through here drop down the field, keeping a hedge and fence on your right, to a gate at the far end.

From here drop down diagonally left towards a stile which takes you out onto the road. Turn left on the road for approximately 270 metres (300 yards) to reach Mire House Farm. (For those of you hoping to detour to Whitley Chapel for a restorative drink the bad news is that the pub indicated on the map closed in the summer of 1996 and the building has been converted into a private house. The next hostelry is at Dipton Mill some 2 kilometres away, so you'd best put your skates on!) Turn right just after the farm, signed to High Staples. Follow the directional arrow along the side of a fence on your right to reach a stile in the far corner. This is a rather boggy area and you may care to cross over right into the next field a little sooner to reach the building at Moss House. Cross over the track and over the stile in the wall ahead. (There is a diversion in the pipeline for this next section which will be waymarked.) In the field aim for a stile in the right hand corner, and once over turn left to reach a plantation. Go over the stile on your left at this point, cross over a stream and turn immediately right to a stile in the fence ahead. Once over, go over the stile on your left (what a carry-on!) and cross the field diagonally right to reach the road – this will no doubt be reached with some relief after the intricacy of these last manoeuvres. Turn right and, after passing High Staples Farm on your left, go through a gateway between the farm and outbuildings, signed to Dye House.

Go through two gates directly ahead of you and out into the fields and drop down diagonally right to reach a gate in the far corner. Keep straight on through a further gate and soon you reach a stile which takes you into the plantation. The enclosed, twilit atmosphere in the woods is in stark contrast to the open fields which you have just left. All is quiet save for an occasional burst of distant birdsong and the gentle murmur of the nearby river. The ground is carpeted with pine needles and the branchless trees soar in vertical lines high up towards the sunlight, reminding one irresistibly of telegraph poles – which may quite possibly be their ultimate fate.

Follow the path through the trees, taking the left track at a fork. At the T-junction which follows turn right and follow the river all the way to Dye House. Soon the houses of this picturesque hamlet come into view.

Turn left on reaching the road to go over the bridge, following the road round the corner past all the houses. At the point where the road turns away right, go straight on along a footpath in front of you and with an accompanying wall on your left. Pass through a kissing gate and straight across the field ahead, walking beneath a very ancient beech tree. Over to your right is a tiny hamlet with the unusual name of Juniper!

Cross over the tarmac road and up the steps ahead where a stile takes you into fields once more. Carry on in the same direction, walking towards Blackhall Wood with a wall now on your right. As you reach the wood a backward glance will show Slaley Forest on the skyline (one of the few large forests in the North Pennines) and

The bridge at Dye House.

Dotland Park

Burntridge Moor which you have just crossed, away to your right. Go through a kissing gate and follow the path round the edge of the wood. A further kissing gate gives access to a field. Follow the fence on your right through two fields. In the third one follow the directional arrows left, skirting the corner of the field to reach a gate which takes you out onto a minor road at GR934595.

Turn left along the road and after roughly 180 metres (200 yards) go over a stile which appears on your right. Go straight on over a ditch and then slightly left over the crest of a hill. Extensive views now open up over towards Hexham and beyond. Walk towards the buildings of Dotland Park which are diagonally left. Your target is the gate in the far left corner of the field – it has a short section of stone wall to the right. Once through the gate follow the good farm track which curves round to the farm buildings. Take the stile to the left of the sheep pens and follow the track once more through the farm buildings. Turn left on reaching the tarmac and follow it over the burn. This is a very pretty spot in springtime when the banks are clothed in daffodils and primroses. Keep on until you reach a minor road at GR933607.

Cross over the road and follow the track opposite which takes you to the road at Diptonmill. The pub here of the same name is a super place for refreshments if you've timed it right. If not, don't blame me but turn right along the road, over the bridge and turn right immediately after Diptonmill Cottage. The track is signed to Hole House and soon leads to a gate with two accompanying stiles. Take the left one and cross the next field keeping close to a plantation on the left. There are many sloe bushes along here which make superb sloe gin if you're that way inclined! Carry on in this same direction to reach Hole House. Follow the path round the right side of the high stone wall, going down the side of a garage and passing behind the house to reach a footbridge. Once over this the very obvious path climbs uphill amongst trees. When you emerge from the trees keep on in the same direction with the plantation on your right initially. Go through three fields and in the final one take the stile in the corner on your right to reach a track and a ruined building. Turn immediately left and climb uphill with a hedge on your left to reach a gate. Just to one side of the gate is a seat in memory of Jim Hobbs who was secretary of Hexham Ramblers for 27 years! This is a superb place to sit and take in the magnificent view back over Slaley Forest with Dipton Wood away to your left.

Carry on uphill through the next field to reach a minor road. Cross over here and go over the stile ahead signed to High Shield. As you reach the next stile Hexham becomes clearly visible below, backed

Hole House.

by the high lands of Hadrian's Wall country. From here it is downhill all the way to the town centre in Hexham.

It is surely one of the most satisfying moments of any walk when you see your final destination laid out before you – particularly if it's downhill! Perhaps this is the moment to reflect on the past two days. Was it only yesterday that you set out from Haltwhistle to discover the historic remains at Vindolanda? Think of Beltingham, that idyllic spot where time appears to have stood still, the drama and beauty of Allen Banks and, after a long day, the charms of Allendale Town and a well deserved rest. Today's walk was quite a contrast as you traversed the high moorland before wandering through undulating farmland and tiny hamlets to reach this, your first sight of journey's end.

Well, the Allendale Amble is almost over but you must continue a little longer yet so, with a hedge and fence on your left, keep dropping downhill all the way until you reach the road at GR936630. Turn right along the road, taking care as the traffic can be quite fast at times. After approximately 360 metres (400 yards) you reach Elvaston Road on your left which is unmarked. This is followed immediately by a red brick house and a narrow gap in the stone wall. This unremarkable opening gives access to the Long Nick which runs straight down to the town and was developed beside a nineteenth-century estate boundary. Go down this, passing vegetable plots initially. For most of its length it is bounded by high stone walls interspersed with hedges and fences; do not be tempted to turn off to the right when an opening appears. The passage goes on for almost 800 metres (½ mile) and took me back to my childhood in Lancashire when we used to run down short passages known as 'ginnels'. (This is a very welcome and unusual lead-in to our destination and an ideal opportunity to indulge in a philosophical discussion on the origins and naming of these urbanised pathways.) Eventually you reach a road where you must turn right, passing British Telecom buildings also on the right. At the end of the street you see another passage in the right hand corner with iron railings in front of it. Go along here, between stone walls once more before reaching some steep steps which take you down to the B6306 road. Turn left here to reach the centre of Hexham. When you reach the main street a right turn will take you to both the bus and train stations. If you've time left to visit the Abbey then any of the streets ahead of you will take you there – the one down the side of the Midland Bank, for example.

Congratulations, you have now completed the Allendale Amble and I hope the experience has been enjoyable and has created a host of pleasant memories to take home with you.

Hexham is a remarkable town which stands on a terrace overlooking the Tyne and is dominated by its Abbey. It is the commercial centre of the area and is a bustling, lively place with plenty to see. Hexham Abbey was founded in Saxon times and during one period was said to be the finest church north of the Alps! The crypt, which dates from AD 674, is one of the finest in Britain and was built with Roman stones from the fort of Corstopitum. Also of Saxon origin is St Wilfred's Chair or Frith Stool which was the Bishop's seat in medieval times when it became a place of sanctuary. The Monk's night stair is not to be missed either. This is still used by the present choir and was the route by which the monks entered the abbey from their dormitory.

The market place beside the abbey houses a slender monument of red sandstone and a long market colonnade which provides shelter for the traders. Hexham received its charter in 1239 but the colonnade, known as the Shambles, was built as a covered market in 1766 by Sir Walter Blackett, Lord of the Manor. This is the scene of the Hexham Riot of 1761 and the last time that blood was shed in the town. The

Hexham Abbey.

Riot Act was read after an angry crowd of mostly Allendale lead miners gathered to object to the regulations regarding military service. About 50 people were killed and 300 injured and for many years the North Yorkshire Militia were known as the Hexham Butchers.

The sandstone monument in the square is of special interest, being ornately decorated and built as a source of water in 1901. It bears a poem to which the newly-arrived walker can easily relate, concerning as it does both drinking water and the site of its origins high in the hills. The inscription, worked in bronze, reads:-

'O YOU WHO DRINK MY COOLING WATERS CLEAR
FORGET NOT THE FAR HILLS FROM WHENCE THEY FLOW
WHERE OVER FELL AND MOORLAND YEAR BY YEAR
SPRING SUMMER AUTUMN WINTER COME AND GO
WITH SHOWERING SUN AND RAIN AND STORM AND SNOW
WHERE OVER THE GREEN BENTS FOREVER BLOW
THE FOUR FREE WINDS OF HEAVEN WHERE TIME FALLS
IN SOLITARY PLACES CALM AND SLOW
WHERE PIPES THE CURLEW AND THE PLOVER CALLS
BENEATH AN OPEN SKY MY WATERS SPRING
BENEATH THE CLEAR SKY WELLING FAIR AND SWEET
A DRAUGHT OF COOLNESS FOR YOUR THIRST TO BRING
A SOUND OF COOLNESS IN THE BUSY STREET'

Wilfred Wilson Gibson Hexham Feb 1901

The Moot Hall, which also stands in the market square, was built in the fourteenth century and was where the Archbishops' Courts were once held; today it houses an exhibition centre. The archway under the hall leads to the Old Gaol (built in 1330) which is now home to the Tourist Information Centre on the ground floor, whilst above it is the Border History Museum. This is a fascinating place which illustrates with displays and audio visual aids the history of the infamous Border Reivers in the fifteen and sixteenth centuries. The Reivers were a law unto themselves and came from all walks of life. They were skilled in cattle rustling, raiding and tracking and were well organised gangsters. For more information on these desperadoes you'll just have to visit the museum yourself!

There is considerably more to see and do in Hexham than can be fitted into the available space here – a visit to the Tourist Information

Centre will provide you with lots more ideas. Accommodation is no problem and there are numerous and varied places in which to eat and drink.

Date walked _____

Companions _____

_____

_____

Weather _____

Highlight of the walk _____

_____

_____

_____

Any other memories _____

_____

_____

WALK NUMBER THREE – CIRCULAR
'MERLIN'S WAY'
Edmundbyers – Stanhope – Edmundbyers

Total distance 52.8 kms (33 miles)
Edmundbyers to Stanhope 28 kms (17.5 miles)
Stanhope to Edmundbyers 24.8 kms (15.5 miles)

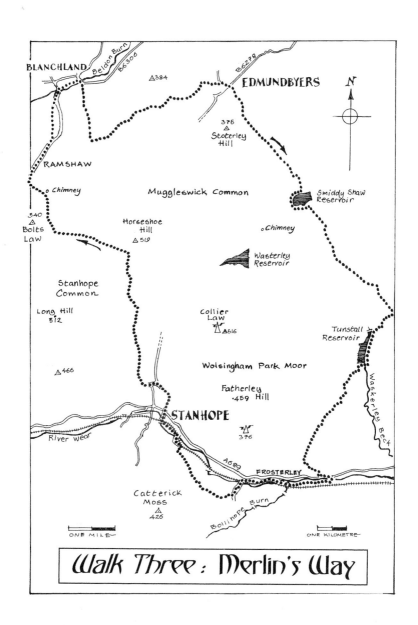

BLANCHLAND

Beldon Burn

B6306

△384

EDMUNDBYERS

B6278

N

RAMSHAW

376
△
Stoterley
Hill

o Chimney

Muggleswick Common

Smiddy Shaw
Reservoir

.540
△
Bolts
Law

Horseshoe
Hill
△519

o Chimney

Wasterley
Reservoir

Stanhope
Common

Long Hill
512

Collier
Law
△516

Tunstall
Reservoir

△466

Wolsingham Park Moor

Fatherley
.459 Hill

STANHOPE

Waskerley Beck

River Wear

376

A689

FROSTERLEY

Catterick
Moss
△
426

Bollihope Burn

ONE MILE

ONE KILOMETRE

Walk Three : Merlin's Way

Walk 3

Day One
Edmundbyers to Stanhope

Distance: 28 kms (17.5 miles)
Ordnance Survey Maps:
1;25,000
  Outdoor Leisure 31-Teesdale
  Pathfinder 571 – Lanchester
1;50,000
  Landranger 87 – Hexham, Haltwhistle & surrounding area
  Landranger 88 – Tyneside & Durham area (just)
  Landranger 92 – Barnard Castle & Richmond

*T*his is an exhilarating walk starting with a climb up onto the heather-clad moors of Muggleswick Common before reaching Smiddy Shaw reservoir with its extensive views. Next comes Waskerley village and its railway associations followed by a delightful elevated stretch along Salter's Ridge. Eventually you lose height as you drop down to Tunstall Reservoir in its idyllic setting. From here farmland is the order of the day as you make your way down to the River Wear. The final stretch follows the line of the river through Frosterley, famous for its 'marble', before finishing at Stanhope, 'Queen of the Dale'. It is a long day with nowhere to stop for refreshments so make sure you pack plenty of provisions in your sac and don't forget your midge repellent – Weardale is renowned for them.

The walk starts in the village of Edmundbyers, thought to be named after Edmund, a ninth-century English king who freed areas of the North of England from the Vikings. Although quite small the village is very popular in the summer months with walkers, cyclists and caravanners. Its close proximity to the Derwent Reservoir may account for part of its popularity. The reservoir, which covers 1,000 acres, lies just north of the village on the boundary between Durham and Northumberland.

Leave Edmundbyers in an easterly direction along the B6278, passing the YHA on your right. Go through the gate immediately after the hostel and walk straight ahead through a second gate and past a field on your right which is a camp site. Follow the path as it drops down towards Burnhope Burn. At the end of a broken wall on your right follow the path for a further 18 metres (20 yards) before forking right on a faint path which drops down to the burn. Cross the wooden bridge and go up the rise ahead, aiming to the left of two telegraph poles. Soon a stile can be seen in the wall ahead. Once over this a path slightly right leads you up a series of steps in the hillside. This may be difficult to locate when the bracken is high so an alternative is to turn right and follow the wall to the two telegraph poles. From here turn left and follow the stream uphill and, approximately halfway up, follow a green path on the left up to the top. Go over the stile and West Cot House comes into view. Go left over a little beck, then swing right and carry on uphill beside the beck to reach another stile. Once over this go across a grassy area to reach the road. This is GR 020495 and West Cot House is on your right.

Turn left along the road towards East Cot House. From here delightful views can be had looking back towards Edmundbyers, whilst Derwent Reservoir can be glimpsed in the far distance. The reservoir is one of the largest of its kind in Britain and is home to many different species of wildfowl. There is a wild life sanctuary with accompanying nature trail, hide and viewing spots and anglers fish for brown and rainbow trout. On another part of the water is a sailing club and the British Windsurfing Championships are held here as well. It's marvellous to think that all these activities can co-habit successfully. On reaching East Cot House, turn right at the end of a sheep compound on your right and follow a fence and then a dry stone wall up the hillside. Keeping the wall on your right, cross over a tarmac road and carry on up the hillside. Take care not to get diverted left but stay close to the wall to reach Lamb Shield Farm. (The hut near the farm looked like a suitable place to shelter when I was researching the walk but I discovered to my cost that it housed a guard dog; needless

Approaching Smiddy Shaw Reservoir.

to say I walked on rather briskly!). Prominent on the skyline over to your left are three cairns known as the Three Curricks.

Press on along a good track as it runs parallel to the wall on your right, ignoring any tracks which swing left. Soon you drop down to enter a boggy area with a well-placed, simple stone bridge over a stream. The path now leads you back to a wall side. Go through an unusual sliding gate construction to enter an area with several grouse butts to the left of you. Continue on with a wall on your right. When the stone wall veers away right it is replaced by a fence. Follow the path alongside the fence to another sliding gate. (The next short section unfortunately does not relate to the OS map very closely as a new fence has appeared since the map was published. The right of way describes a straight line which is now impossible to follow.) Pass through the sliding gate and continue with the wall on your right until it meets a fence in 54 metres (60 yards). Turn left with the fence and follow for 90 metres (100 yards) and then follow it right. The fence soon becomes a wall. Shortly afterwards, go over a stile of sorts and continue with the wall on your right; eventually, we begin dropping down towards Hisehope Burn until another sliding gate is reached. Continue through this until a track is met coming in from the left from Birkhot Farm; go through the gate in the wall on the right and turn immediately left to follow the wall down to Hisehope Burn. This is a delightful spot, quite sheltered and isolated from the remote peat moorland away to your right, where the burn has its source high up on Hisehope Head some 3 kilometres distant.

Make your way over the burn and climb the hillside ahead alongside a fence on the left with Backstsone Burn deep in the gorge on your right. Follow the fence as it turns sharp left to reach a metal gate about 180 metres (200 yards) along. (GR043471.)

Turn right here heading towards a sluice gate on the wall of Smiddy Shaw Reservoir which can be seen on the skyline approximately 800 metres (½ mile) away. In mist a compass bearing of 161 degrees is useful as the paths where they do exist are intermittent. Make your way as best you can until you reach an overflow pipe from the reservoir, the surround of which is dated 1872. Go past this up the slope to a plateau where 80 stone steps are conveniently placed to aid your passage up the final embankment to the reservoir. Here you meet a good track which you follow right to Smiddy Shaw House.

There are extensive views from this elevated position back towards the Three Curricks whilst to the right of them is Derwentside with the Roman Wall country in the far distance. Smiddy Shaw reservoir was once part of a unique area of ancient Caledonian Pine and during the summers of 1976 and 1977, when the water was at its lowest, large stumps of pine were revealed.

Stay on this excellent track as it circumvents the reservoir until you are almost directly opposite your entry point. At this crossing of tracks take the one directly ahead which soon curves away right to reach a road at GR047457. (The building visible diagonally left is the Moorcock pub.) Turn left along the road for a hundred yards to reach a sign directing you right on the Waskerley Way. Follow this to Waskerley village, passing a church on your right which is well hidden amongst the trees. At the entrance to the churchyard are elaborate iron gates with a crest WM 1897 on them. The track turns left and then right to reach a picnic area on the Waskerley Way.

The first building you have just passed has a connection with Dr Who – did you spot it? Waskerley was once a working railway village in the middle of the nineteenth century with a church, chapel, shops and a school, apart from the necessary railway buildings which included wagon repair shops and a shed for 6 engines. Quite a large community existed here at 354 metres above sea level, until the railway

Waskerley Church.

went into decline with the closure of the lead mines and the opening of less complicated railway lines. It eventually closed in 1968–9.

Leave the picnic area via a gate taking you onto the old railway line.

This section of line is the terminus of a slope coming up from Hownsgill, known as Nanny Mayer's Incline and named after Mrs Mayer, the landlady of the Moorcock pub mentioned earlier.

Turn left along the line for approximately 90 metres (100 yards) where a track crosses your path beside a gate and just prior to a barn. Turn right here and follow the track to a fence and then a gate. Negotiate the gate and follow the fence on your left until it turns left towards an old ruined barn. Leave the fence and walk over the rise aiming for two gates in the far left-hand corner of the field. Go over the stile to the right of the gate directly ahead of you (not the one to your left) and go out onto the open moor. Walk diagonally left on a grassy track towards Drypry Plantation. As you near it a vague path branches right towards the corner of the plantation and a perimeter fence, follow this to the corner and then follow the path downhill with the fence on your left. It looks remarkably like something from

World War II and in fact it is, the plantation once housed one of the largest ammunitions dumps in the country.

A little further on the path turns left again and you must follow it, over a stile. The route is now alongside the fence and plantation for just over 1.6 kilometres (1 mile). In high summer the bracken can make for rather heavy going but there are compensations in the lovely views over Wolsingham Park Moor with Tunstall Reservoir prominent in the distance. This is your next destination and the half-way point of the day. After approximately 1.2 kilometres (¾ mile) you reach a clearing where you need to keep straight on, soon to rejoin the fence and plantation At long last a stile appears which takes you out into open ground. Here the official route goes high up left, hugging the plantation for the last time to reach a wall at the far side of the field. Here you turn left with the trees and then immediately right along an old green lane (GR 069434). After approximately 90 metres (100 yards), turn right at the corner of a broken-down wall and follow a stream downhill to reach a good track where you turn left. (However, from the stile mentioned above, a clear obvious grassy track can be seen straight ahead of you, a short distance away from the dry stone wall on your right. This crosses the field and goes through the remains of an old gateway before shortly meeting a good track coming in from the right. A left turn here and the track soon meets the tiny stream which the official route has followed downhill. This is certainly a more direct line.) Keep on the track for approximately 45 metres (50 yards) and then at a broken-down wall follow a vague path diagonally right. Keep along the contour line as you traverse Salter's Ridge which, from its name, we can assume was the site of an old salt road carrying that expensive commodity from the ships at South Shields.

From the ridge you are looking down to Weardale, one of England's highest settled dales. The forest of Weardale, which stretched from Eastgate (higher up the valley) to the Cumbrian border, was the hunting ground for the Bishop of Durham. This is the land of the Prince Bishops, the Counts Palatine, who were created to protect England from the marauding Scots and enforce rule in a troubled Northern Area. They ruled from 1080 until 1836 over County Durham and much of Northumberland and their main seat was at Bishop Auckland further down the Wear Valley. They had extensive powers, second only to the king's and their influence can be seen everywhere from their great palaces to some of the earliest mine workings.

Go over a track which crosses your path, keeping the same direction and passing a fenced-off copse of trees higher up the hill. (If you lose sight of the path along this section just keep parallel with the dry stone wall away to your left.) The other side of the wall is a disused railway line. This was built by the Stockton and Darlington Railway Company about 1845 and was linked to the line at Waskerley and very probably built on the old salt road. Eventually you reach a gate in the wall ahead, pass through here and a little further on you meet two isolated wooden gate posts. Once through these keep straight on ignoring any paths which fork left up towards the wall. After approximately 140 metres (160 yards) you reach a crossing of paths in line with a small gate which is waymarked in the wall away to your left. Turn right here on a vague path which soon starts dropping down towards the reservoir, parallel with a raised mound on your left. There are stunning views of Tunstall Reservoir in the sheltered valley below, nestling beneath the high moors.

This scenic gem, owned by Northumberland Water, lies in the valley of Waskerley Beck on the edge of Wolsingham Park Moor. Around its banks is a host of plants and animals; kestrel, cuckoo, spotted woodpecker and song thrush are just a few of the birds which can be seen there whilst at its northern end is a nature reserve created to protect wetland plants, including the nationally rare Thread Rush. On the western shore is a car park, picnic area and fishing lodge where the fishermen record their catches; fly fishing only as the reservoir is stocked only with trout.

Soon you reach a waymarked gate and stile (your route is waymarked now all the way to the reservoir). Once through here follow the path as it curves round left above a tiny valley before reaching the edge of a plantation. Go left here with the waymark, immediately after crossing a tiny burn. The path becomes very obvious now as you descend. Eventually you re-cross that tiny burn again to reach a gate across a track to the reservoir bridge. Turn right through here and go over the stile immediately on your left (rather a grand affair) and follow the footpath through Backstone Bank Wood.

This is coppiced oak from the sixteenth century and is now an SSSI (Site of Special Scientific Interest), full of fascinating birds including warblers and pied flycatchers. The wood, originally part of Wolsingham Park, was owned by the Bishop of Durham and by 1331 the estate had two park-keepers to look after the trees and deer; the roe deer is a shy animal which is active between dusk and dawn. The trees were coppiced to provide timber for charcoal which was used as a fuel for lead smelting.

This excellent path along the east side of the reservoir makes for delightful walking with many glimpses of the water through the trees and possibly of the fishermen either along the banks or out on the water.

At the far end the path climbs uphill slightly to join a broader track coming in from the left; turn right along it, passing through two impressive stone pillars before dropping down to a bridge over the weir. Follow the dam wall which has conveniently placed benches along it suitable for a late lunch perhaps, before reaching Foresters Lodge Cottage and the road. Turn left here and after approximately 55 metres (60 yards) turn right at the first footpath sign. Go over the stile and cross the field following the direction of the waymark to a gate which soon becomes visible ahead of you. Pass through this gate and across a stream (note some old stone farm buildings on your left) and a stile followed by a further gate. This gives access to a field; walk diagonally right up this field to reach a stone stile in the wall

Tunstall Reservoir.

ahead. Carry on once again diagonally right to reach a gateway. Go through this and continue with a wall and fence on your right. At the farm track turn right.

Go along this track to a T-junction just before a Dutch barn; ignore the track which goes off left to the farmhouse. Turn left at the T-junction and follow this track to pass through a gate at Jofless Cottage at the end of the field. Keep on the track across the next field and through the gate. Turn right almost immediately here and follow the wall uphill. At the top of the field turn left through a gate and onto a green lane which skirts a plantation on your right. As you go higher Wolsingham comes into view away to your left. This is a delightful town of wonderful warm stone buildings and home to England's oldest agricultural show which has been in existence for 200 years.

All too soon the green track comes to an end as you pass through a gate into an area of ruined buildings known as Park Wall. A vague track goes diagonally right through the ruins to a gateway. Turn left here across a narrow field and through a further gateway. Follow the rutted track in a south-westerly direction to a copse of trees. At the copse do not follow the directional arrow left through a gateway (this drops down to Wolsingham) but keep straight on with the wall on your left initially, then aim for a stone wall at the far end of the field. The ground here can be a bit of a quagmire in wet weather so pick your way across until you come to a gate and firmer ground at last. Once through the gateway, turn left; from this vantage point you will notice a group of farm buildings known as Ladley in the fields above the wood. This is your next destination.

Drop down through the gorse towards Ladley Wood and an obvious opening in the stone wall. Once through here, turn right alongside the forest with the wall on your right. About 18 metres (20 yards) before the end of this wall turn left, following the edge of the coniferous plantation downhill with a little burn on your right. As you drop down towards Thornhope Beck you meet a fire-break across your path. Turn right here across some rough stepping stones over the burn and then turn immediately left, dropping down more steeply to a footbridge over Thornhope Beck GR 049386.

This is a delightful spot in springtime with the trees emblazoned with golden yellow catkins. Follow the directional arrows left up the wooden steps to come out into the fields once more. Leave the fence at a right angle and strike uphill towards the farm buildings mentioned earlier which soon become visible. The farmhouse is sadly empty but has commanding views back over Wolsingham and the Weardale valley.

Pass between the house and buildings, keep on in the same direction uphill, across the field to find a stile in the wall ahead. Cross the corner of the next field to a further stile. Keep the same direction diagonally left over the crest of the hill and soon Newlands Hall comes into view below you. (As you descend the hill look out for a distinctive group of trees on the far horizon. These are known locally as the Elephant Trees due to their supposed resemblance to a line of elephants). Drop down to a gate, cross another field to a further gate which in turn leads you onto a track through the farm buildings. Follow the arrows through the farmyard with the house on your right. Turn right, around the last building, ignoring the arrows pointing westwards and drop downhill on the concrete farm road. Carry on along the farm road for a short distance until you reach a track going off to your left (if you reach a cattle grid you've gone too far!). Turn left along the track until you reach a gate, once through here leave the track and walk diagonally right across a field towards the far corner. Here you'll find two gates, go through the one on the right and follow a fence on your left as you drop down towards the A689. At the bottom of the field turn left through another gate (ignoring the one straight ahead of you) and then turn immediately right to go over a burn. On the other side of the burn turn left and follow it all the way to a stile which takes you out onto the road.

Turn left along the road for approximately 360 metres (400 yards) and then turn right down a road signed to a caravan site. Follow the road as it passes over the River Wear and then swings right to follow the river upstream. Although this 800 metres (½ mile) to the site is metalled there is a very wide grass verge which makes for pleasant walking. At the caravan site follow the road as it turns right, leaving it as it swings left, to reach a footpath beside the river.

This is delightful walking beside the River Wear, which has its birth high up the valley at Wearhead where Killhope Burn and Burnhope Burn meet. There are many wild flowers along the banks including the yellow and brown Mimulus flower, known as the monkey-flower.

After passing the static caravans a railway line becomes your companion for much of the route to Frosterley.

The railway arrived in Frosterley in 1847, built to transport limestone from the hills around Stanhope down to Tyneside where it was used to remove impurities in the iron- and steel-making process.

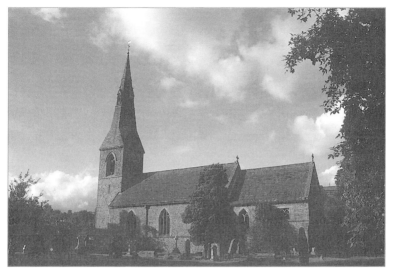

Frosterley Church.

When you reach the road, turn right to cross the river again and then fork left immediately across a concreted area with a large industrial building on it. Straight ahead and to the left of a group of trees is a footpath, bounded on the left by a tall metal fence. Follow this to a minor road and turn left along it to go through an area known as The Batts. Keep straight on, passing allotments on your left followed by a large brick building on your right.

You are now on the outskirts of Frosterley, famous for its 'marble', which is in fact a particularly beautiful form of dark limestone. In it the fossils of plants and animals millions of years old can be seen clearly. It has been used as a decorative material in churches since medieval times and can be seen in the doorway of Frosterley church, (just ahead of you) on the chancel floor of Wolsingham church, extensively in Durham Cathedral and at Auckland Palace Chapel. Frosterley, known in earlier times as 'Forest Lea', was another forest area used for deer hunting, and the hunters would meet in the hostel now called The Foresters Arms where, during re-building, bows and arrows were found in the earth.

The path leads once again to the railway track. On reaching a gate and metalled road on your right, go through the gate and follow the tarmac, forking left as the road veers right and passing 'Appletrees' house on your left. Follow the directional arrows left through two gates and alongside the vicarage wall. At a fork in the path, follow the left one downhill over a little bridge and then up to meet the road. Before reaching the road, our path passes a number of rows of cottages and gardens on our right; their gardens continue to the left, dropping down delightfully into the wooded valley below.

At the road turn left immediately down the minor road signed to Egglestone and Middleton-in-Tees, dropping down to the bridge over the River Wear. (Just before the bridge is the Black Bull Inn which serves food as well as real ale.) Once over the bridge you pass The Old Sunday School Guesthouse on your left which has a tea-room! Carry on up the hill and when you reach another school on your left, look for a footpath sign opposite. Cross the road through the gate and follow the path uphill keeping an accompanying hedge on your left. Go through a gateway and keep on uphill towards a large gate. Go through here and follow the hedge as it swings away left. Carry on uphill and at the top of the field at (GR 018363) turn right, ignoring the stile which takes you higher up the hill. At the corner of this field go through a gate and follow the wall on your right to reach some buildings. Pass between them to emerge onto a metalled road and carry on past Dryburn Side Cottage to a gate and a Weardale Way sign.

Negotiate the gate and drop down diagonally right towards Peak

Above Frosterley.

Parson Byers.

Field Farm. Turn left through an old gateway and in approximately 90 metres (100 yds) turn right through a gateway to follow the track towards the farm. In a few yards, cross a burn (a footbridge is available if needed). A short distance away from the farmhouse the track veers left through another gateway. Follow this and keep straight across the next field with Dry Burn on your left. Go over a stone step-stile and across another field and stile, then in the third field walk uphill towards a spoil heap and cross over a stile well to the right of this heap and to the left of a gate. In the next field aim for a pile of ruined buildings at the far end, passing a disused quarry on your left. Pass through a gate and turn right on a track in front of the ruins until you reach the corner of the ruined building. From here walk diagonally downhill left to reach a stile in the far corner. Once over this, go left across the next field, keeping a short distance from the wall until you reach a stile in the wall ahead. Once over here look for a gate in a wall on the skyline directly ahead. Cross this field in the same direction towards a natural gap in the trees lining the beck and go over Cow

Burn at the bottom which should be waymarked. Continue uphill in the same direction to reach our gate which is situated in the wall corner. Stanhope should now be visible from this vantage point.

Go over the stile adjacent to the gate and carry on in the same general direction over the brow of a hill. The buildings of Parson Byers soon come into view. Continue to a gate by a telegraph pole; in a few yards cross a farm track and through two gates in quick succession to reach the farm buildings. (A marvellous Monkey Puzzle tree can be seen in front of the farm, making a stark contrast against the stonework of the old building.) Ignore the track heading off right which leads down to the main road and go through the gate ahead of you. Follow a line of telegraph poles down to a minor road. If you look carefully on the ground you may notice stones marking the edge of an old paved trod which possibly was used by the miners on their way to work from the cottages you are approaching. Turn left on the road and follow it past a caravan site (the backpackers amongst you will need to stop here, just 800 metres short of Stanhope) otherwise go down to a bridge over the railway and then another one over the river.

Take the Weardale Way footpath sign on your left, straight after crossing the river bridge. The Weardale Way is a long distance path of some 113 kilometres running from the North Sea at Wearmouth to Wearhead and the birth of the River Wear. Follow the path beside the river, passing a large factory on your right. This looks rather out of place against the dramatic fellside but brings much-needed work to the area. On reaching the railway line cross with care! Although to all intents and purposes the line is disused, the occasional steam train has been known to run along here.

In 1993 the Weardale Railway Society was formed to help save the line. Its objectives are initially to protect the section from Bishop Auckland to Eastgate (a few miles west of Stanhope) and also to support the company formed to bring the line back into operation. The hope is that, apart from becoming a major tourist attraction, it would eventually be developed as a regular public transport service. If it could attract freight users as well the rewards would be even greater, helping to alleviate the congestion on the country roads.

Once over the line, cross the next field to a kissing gate in the middle of the wall ahead. Keep on in the same direction to pass through a further kissing gate and the final field. Re-cross the railway line and follow the lane past some delightful cottages. At the T-junction turn

Stanhope stepping stones.

right up the hill to reach the square in Stanhope. To your left is Stanhope Castle, built in 1798 on the site of a medieval castle and restored in 1875. It has had many uses, as a museum, shooting lodge, approved school and now as up-market apartments. Sadly, recent additions have marred its appearance and it is best viewed from across the river.

Stanhope is the capital of the upper dale and is a lively place with ample accommodation, shops and pubs. Unfortunately for backpackers the caravan site is only for statics. On the opposite side of the square is a cafe which, if you're lucky, may still be open. Just past the parish church is the Durham Dales Centre, which houses another cafe, Tourist Information Centre and craft shops. This area was all part of the castle gardens which were originally laid out with fruit, flower and vegetable gardens and included heated greenhouses for growing figs and grapes. The only remnant of those days is the Gazebo with its tower, which is in the Dales Centre grounds and was built in 1875 for Henry Pease, owner of the castle.

Stanhope Church with its Norman tower dates from the twelfth century and is home to a Roman altar found on Bollihope Common in 1747, but this can only be seen by special request. In the churchyard, just inside the gate, stand the remains of the old market cross which was superseded by one erected in 1871 and which is just outside the gates. A Friday market was held in the town from the early twelfth century but ceased to exist in the early twentieth. On the churchyard wall itself is something quite remarkable, a 250 million year old fossil tree which was found in a quarry in 1962. It originally grew in a forest near Edmundbyers Cross, close to the road over from Stanhope. As it decayed, sand formed around it making a perfect cast.

Stanhope Hall, approximately 800 metres (½ mile) west of the church along the A689, is an impressive fortified manor house and now in use as a hotel. It is home to the story of the Stanhope Fairies who supposedly cast a spell on one of the family's daughters. She had wandered into the fairies' cave and, having seen them dancing, was forever in their power. To break the spell the house had to be kept in total silence for one night. Of course these things never go according to plan and the daughter's pet dog barked as the fairies passed and all was lost! If you like a happy ending there are those who say that the father got his daughter back by answering three riddles set by the Fairy King. As you can see Stanhope has lots to offer if you've the time to spare and is certainly worth a return visit.

Stanhope Castle.

Walk 3

Day Two
Stanhope to Edmundbyers

Distance 24.8 kms (15.5 miles)
Ordnance Survey Maps:
1:25,000
Outdoor Leisure 31 – Teesdale (just)
    Pathfinder 560 – Allendale Town & Blanchland (just)
    Pathfinder 561 – Consett (tiny pt.)
    Pathfinder 570 – Allenheads & Rookhope
    Pathfinder 571 – Lanchester (just)
1:50,000
    Landranger 87 – Hexham, Haltwhistle & surrounding area
    Landranger 92 – Barnard Castle & Richmond (just)

After the initial easy walk through Stanhope Burn Dene the route follows the burn up into remote moorland, so map and compass are essential. A brisk climb takes you out of the valley onto the old railway track which you follow for a mile or so before crossing Burnhope Head. There are constant reminders of the old lead mining days in this first half of the walk. The descent to Ramshaw and more lush pastures comes as a sharp contrast after the exposed moorland; the contrast is heightened on reaching the memorable village of Blanchland, the highlight of the whole walk. From here another brisk climb over Buckshott Fell takes you onto Edmundbyers Common and the final few kilometres across this heather clad moor to the end.

Leave Stanhope via the square, taking the road between 'The Bonny Moor Hen' pub and the church. This was the scene of the notorious

'Battle of Stanhope' where starving miners fought for the right to poach the bonny moor hen (the red grouse). The victory of the miners over the keepers resulted in the pub's new name and in a song:

'Oh, the miners of Weardale they are all valiant men,
They will fight till they die for the bonny moor hen'.

Climb the hill and turn left at the top, past Stanhope Methodist Church and School on your right. Take the walled track immediately after this, just before the driveway to the bungalow. Pass through a little gate further up the track and carry on straight up the hillside. Cross over a farmer's track and keep climbing, taking care not to be diverted left into the quarry. Carry on over two bridges with Crawley Edge looming directly ahead of you. After going over the metal stile, follow the fence and then a wall on your left all the way to Crawley Side. There are excellent views along here into the old limestone quarry workings and away to the fells beyond.

Soon you reach the road at Crawley Side where you turn left for approximately 450 metres (500 yards) to reach a sharp left hand bend in the road and with Lane Head Farm on your right. Drop down right here between hawthorn trees to reach a tarmac road which will take you all the way to the quarry head.

Stanhope Church.

The area is full of disused mine workings which are a constant reminder of past times when the area contained a lead smelting works, iron ore furnaces and limekilns. It has now been colonised by a profusion of trees and plants and mysterious pools have formed at the base of the sheer cliff walls. The pools house a host of insect life while birds nest happily on the cliff ledges. It always amazes me how frequently nature, when left to her own devices, takes charge once more and creates something beautiful from the devastation left by man's industry.

At the quarry head keep straight on past the buildings where Heathery Burn comes in from the right.

It was here that in 1843 workmen found a cave containing an incredible collection of Bronze Age tools and weapons. This was the finest collection of the period ever found in the United Kingdom and included bronze spearheads, a bronze bucket, amber necklaces, a gold bracelet and other objects which suggested the early use of domestic horses and wheeled vehicles. One theory is that a well-to-do family took shelter in the cave when the river was in flood and subsequently drowned. The cave is no longer there and the hoard, known as the Heathery Burn Collection, is now housed in the British Museum in London.

When the road curves away left over the burn GR986414 go straight ahead over a gate, with Stanhope Burn on your left. Once over the gate take the slightly higher path, which starts off as a green track, and follow the burn for approximately 800 metres (½ mile). At GR986422 there is a small stone in the ground and a break in the raised bank. The official right of way is left here to the river, across it and along the other side and back over again at a sharp bend in Stanhope Burn at GR987426. However, you may wish to follow in the footsteps of countless others and carry on along the same side of the river to reach the bend. Just prior to the bend you will have to climb uphill a little where the ground has fallen away. Once round this obstacle, cross over East Whiteley Burn which comes in from the right and keep on along the right side of Stanhope Burn for 100 metres until you reach a track crossing your path just before some old sheds. Turn right uphill along the track and just before it swings away to the left you must leave it and turn left along a shallow depression (no path visible at first but you are now following the line of Stanhope Burn in the valley away to your left). Soon a more obvious grassy path appears between the bracken. After just over 400 metres (¼ mile) the path drops down left to the junction of West Whiteley Burn on your right and Stanhope Burn; turn right here over a bridge of sorts to cross Whiteley Burn. This is a lovely sheltered spot, making it ideal for a break if needed. Once over the burn go through a gate directly opposite you which is waymarked and initially follow a green track upwards, leaving it to reach a dry stone wall on your left. Keep alongside the wall, going past a gate and carry on up the hill towards Steward Shield Farm which was once part of a medieval enclosure.

This is a wonderful, remote area which is home to many birds of prey, including the sparrowhawk. We spent quite a while one summer's day watching one as it hovered above the ground in search of food. A bird of prey I would dearly love to see is the Merlin – the smallest of our British falcons – maybe you will have better luck than I. Merlin the magician received his name from this little bird because of its habit of appearing suddenly as if by magic. This special falcon flies low over the ground with frequent changes of direction and feeds on small birds including pipits and larks. Its haunts are the moors where it nests amongst the heather and the North Pennines are its last stronghold. There are magnificent views from here back over Stanhope Common and beyond.

At the next gate on your left, which is waymarked, turn through it and cross the field and through a further gate in the right-hand corner of the field. Follow the rough track which goes uphill through a further gate, passing the farm buildings on your left. Keep straight on, eventually to reach a cattle grid and a road. Keep on this road as it rises steeply towards the mast on Horseshoe Hill. At least there used to be a mast but it was taken down in November 1997 (presumably surplus to requirements). When you're almost at the top you'll reach a path which crosses the road at GR984444 and is in fact a dismantled railway. Turn left onto this path which soon becomes an excellent track; in all, we will follow it for just over 2.4 kilometres (1½ miles). This is superb walking with fine panoramic views away to your left.

The railway line was originally owned by The Weardale Iron Company and ran from Slitt Woods near Westgate to Weatherhill above Stanhope where it connected with the Stanhope and Tyne Railway. It was finally closed about 1940. Workers came from all over the country to work in the lead mines, such was the vast mineral wealth of the area. The work was gruelling, dangerous and unhealthy, for the poisonous dust from the workings infected the miners' lungs and most died in their early forties. They needed enormous strength and willpower to work and survive in the harsh conditions. There were no amenities and many had to walk miles to work each day. Most of them had a plot of land on which to grow vegetables and this helped to feed them and their families; many of these plots still punctuate the landscape. A large proportion of the men worked in remote areas and so had to live in 'mine shops' at the mines, only returning home every weekend or even every other one. To fully appreciate the life of a miner and his family a visit to Killhope, high up the dale is a 'must'. The Lead Mining Centre there actually takes visitors into a mine to experience the working conditions, whilst on the surface are the washing sheds and other exhibitions. Most impressive of all is the 10.3 metres high water wheel which dominates that part of the dale.

After approximately 1.2 kilometres (¾ mile) a clear track comes in from the right. Keep straight on here. Shortly after the railway track goes through a small cutting a fence comes in from the right and follows the line of your track about 45 metres (50 yards) distant. At GR958451 another fence comes in at right-angles to join this one; at this point a tall post marks the position of a stile. Bolt's Law hill at 450 metres high is visible ahead of you and the railway track can be seen starting to curve away left. Leave the railway track here and cross a boggy area to reach the stile. Once over the stile follow the fence on your right along a rather vague path. When the fence turns away right, keep straight on along a broad gully which is just off to your right. You are aiming for the left one of two tall chimneys ahead. In mist take a compass bearing on this chimney which is marked on the 1:50000 OS map.

This gully, believe it or not, is the former railway line which carried coal to power the Sikehead Steam engine used at the mines just beyond the chimney ahead of you. The chimney to the right is known as Jeffrey's Chimney, the culmination of a mile-long flue which took the sulphur fumes away from the dales and made for a healthier environment for the workers. A bonus of the flues was that a valuable amount of lead was deposited along them and young lads were employed to scrape these deposits from the sides. (The effect on those lads' health doesn't bear thinking about.)

At the end of the gully is a marker post and a crossing of tracks. The track going left will take you up onto Bolt's Law from where on a clear day five counties are visible. Just a short way along the one to your right is a solitary pine tree, the only one visible for miles.

This is also the Lead Mining Trail which runs from Cowshill to Edmundbyers and follows part of the route used by the packhorse carriers when crossing the moors. Prior to the advent of railways the main form of transport was the packhorse; these sturdy Galloway ponies carried the lead ore from the mines to the smelt mills. The lead took the form of ingots or 'pigs', weighing about 60 kilos and slung each side of the horse's saddle.

Keep straight on at this crossing towards the chimney. Go over the stile which is before and to the left of the chimney and drop down through the field to reach a gate in the right-hand corner of the field. Once through here make your way slightly left away from the fence on your right, over some rough ground to reach a gate at the bottom of the field. Go through the gate and drop down towards Ramshaw. A further gate takes you through a quarried area and a right turn

Ramshaw village.

here leads you along the quarry track to a gateway and a junction. The Whiteheaps Mine was a hive of industry in its day. A water wheel 13.5 metres in diameter existed here and a little further along the valley was a 15 metres one at Jeffery's Mine. Both were worked from a supply of water from the Sikehead Dams beneath Jeffrey's chimney. In later years fluorspar was mined but this ceased in 1988. The mine is now being cleared and the site is to be reclaimed and returned to nature. Go straight over the junction along the road and up to a fork. Turn right along the Stanhope road through the hamlet of Ramshaw. Follow the road for approximately 1.2 kilometres (¾ mile).

After passing a mine uphill on your right, and just before the road swings away to the left at GR958482, is a track and a large gate on your left. Go through the gate and drop down, passing a ruined building in the field on your right. Soon the path curves to the right and then drops downhill towards the forest. But your route is right here following a footpath sign which is partially hidden beside an overgrown wall and fence on your right. Follow this overgrown path which runs along the edge of the forest initially before gradually dropping down amongst the trees. On reaching a fork take the right hand path which eventually emerges onto a good forest track. Turn right here and follow it all the way to the road where you turn left to reach the tiny village of Baybridge. This delightful village straddles two counties, County Durham and Northumberland and there are two imposing road signs declaring this fact. Just over the road bridge is a car park and picnic area which may be of some use (the local bird population is very friendly but it's only cupboard love) or you may prefer to press on to Blanchland which is only 800 metres (½ mile) away where there are shops, cafe and a hotel.

After crossing the road bridge, take the footpath on your right which follows the River Derwent all the way to Blanchland. This is a well-walked path and is a delight at any time of the year. Very soon the rooftops of Blanchland come into view. At the bridge, your route lies over the bridge itself and up the hill but spare a few minutes to walk the few yards left into the centre of Blanchland. You won't be disappointed; it's a place not to be missed, definitely the highlight of the walk!

My first visit to Blanchland was on a cold, crisp February day; few cars were about to spoil the scene and its effects on me were dramatic, stopping me in my tracks and making me feel as if I'd stepped through Alice's looking glass back into another age. Blanchland means white land and was so-called after the white habits worn by the monks of the Premonstratensian Order who settled here in the twelfth century and founded the abbey on land given to them by Sir Walter de Bolbec. The fifteenth-century gatehouse, in part now occupied by the Post Office, was used by the lay brethren to enter and leave the abbey whilst the Lord Crewe Arms was once the Abbot's Lodge. Inside in the Hilyard Room is a huge fireplace with a priesthole; this was where Tom Forster, leader of the local Jacobites, evaded capture by the King's forces during the uprising of 1715. The lawns at the back of the hotel were once the Abbey cloisters and the Chapter House.

The large gravelled courtyard surrounded by restored cottages was rebuilt by the Lord Crewe Trustees in the eighteenth century and includes some of the walls of the monk's refectory, dormitories and workshops. The abbey church is a wonderful mixture of old and new. The 'new' was built in 1721 by the same trustees when the gaps between the ruins of the old church were filled in. There is so much history and beauty in Blanchland that it's a place to which I'm sure you'll want to return.

Leave Blanchland, crossing the bridge and going up the road as it climbs steeply and at the brow of the hill you'll see a road going off

Blanchland.

Leaving Blanchland.

to the right. Turn right here by the Blanchland sign and follow it for 400 metres (¼ mile). In summer and autumn the dog rose – *Rosa canina* – grows wild in the hedgerows here, its single cupped flowers followed later by beautiful, big rosehips. As you gain height Derwent Reservoir can clearly be seen away to your left and you realise that you've almost come full circle.

When the road turns sharp right, go through the gate ahead of you and climb the fellside. It's a long haul to the top of Buckshott Fell but the views are magnificent. Your path is made easier because of a Land Rover track which you follow right over the top. Shortly afterwards, another broad track comes in from the right, then the ground starts to drop downhill and at GR971481 you will meet the Lead Miners Trail also coming in from the right. Go through a gate on your left which is waymarked and follow this trail which will take you across the common, all the way to Edmundbyers, approximately 4.8 kilometres (3 miles) distant. As you walk along this track a clump of trees and buildings will come into view on your right. This is Pedam's Oak, named after a thief called Pedam who stole the farmers' cattle and sheep and escaped capture by living inside a huge, hollow oak tree. His memory lives on in a poem written by a local nineteenth-century poet called Barras.

Eventually you reach a gate on your right marked Lead Miner's Trail; go through here and turn left and follow the direction of the

Buckshott Fell.

waymark siightly off to the right at GR 978485. The path is obvious
on the ground and runs parallel to a fence as it goes over the hill and
then drops down to reach a gate in the far right-hand corner of the
field. Keep straight on along a grassy path which in late August is a
sheer delight with deep purple heather all around you. This is another
old pack-horse track, one of many which criss-cross the moors in the
North Pennines and which were abandoned with the onset of the
railways and properly engineered roads. The moors are managed as
a habitat for grouse these days, the heather being burnt to encourage
young shoots which are food to the ground nesting birds.

   After a time the path starts to descend and the outskirts of
Edmundbyers come into view. As the path winds its way across the
common, the road from Stanhope can be seen over to your right as
it descends from a height of 476 metres high on Feldon Plain where
lie the remains of Edmundbyers Cross. When you reach the road at
GR014501 turn sharp right downhill and take the first road off to
your left which brings you into Edmundbyers and to the pub.

There's a Post Office-cum-shop in the village which is open every
day, a pub which does food and accommodation, a Youth Hostel,
B&Bs and a camp site. Edmundbyers is a pretty village with its houses
fringing large village greens sloping towards the church. The Church
of St Edmund has some interesting woodwork gathered from churches
throughout the area. Of special interest is the altar which is formed
of a single slab of stone. This style was forbidden in 1571 when it was
removed and subsequently lost for over 300 years. It came to light in
1855 when it was returned to its rightful place. Beyond the church

lies a turnpike bridge and the remains of a lead-smelting mill; the ruins of its flue can be seen up the fellside. The hostel was built in 1600 when it was known as the Low House Inn and is reputed to be haunted by the ghost of a former landlord who died of exposure whilst searching the moors for his missing wife.

Well now you've completed 'Merlin's Way', I hope you've enjoyed the experience and were fortunate to have good weather and extensive views. Go and celebrate – you deserve it.

Date Walked   _____

Companions   _____

_____

_____

Weather   _____

Highlight of the walk   _____

_____

_____

_____

Any other memories   _____

_____

_____

(

WALK NUMBER FOUR – CIRCULAR
'MELMERBY MEANDER'
Lazonby – Melmerby – Lazonby

Total distance 37.6 kms (23.5 miles)
Lazonby to Melmerby 23.2 kms (14.5 miles)
Melmerby to Lazonby 14.4 kms (9 miles)

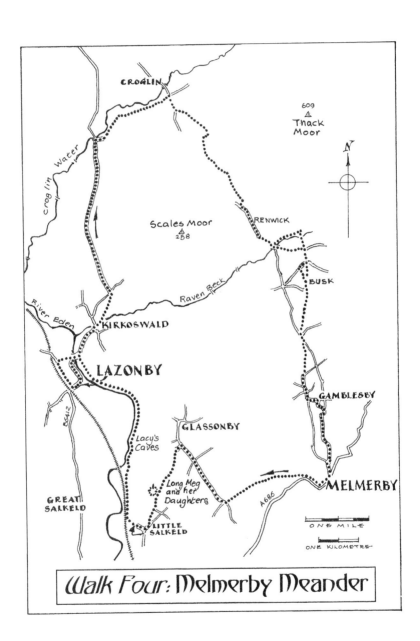

CROGLIN

609
△
Thack
Moor

N

Croglin Water

Scales Moor
△
258

RENWICK

BUSK

Raven Beck

River Eden

KIRKOSWALD

LAZONBY

GAMBLESBY

B5412

GLASSONBY

Lacy's
Caves

Long Meg
and her
Daughters

MELMERBY

A686

GREAT
SALKELD

LITTLE
SALKELD

ONE MILE

ONE KILOMETRE

Walk Four: Melmerby Meander

Walk 4

Day One
Lazonby to Melmerby

Distance 23.2 kms (14.5 miles)
Ordnance Survey Map
1:25,000
    Pathfinder 568 – Southwaite & Kirkoswald (Cumbria)
    Pathfinder 569 – Alston
    Pathfinder 577 – Penrith (North) (Tiny pt.)
    Pathfinder 578 – Appleby-in-Westmorland
1:50,000
    Landranger 86 – Haltwhistle Bewcastle & Alston area.
    Landranger 90 – Penrith & Keswick (Tiny pt.)
    Landranger 91 – Appleby.

*F*armland is the order of the day as you venture into the fertile Eden valley. The walking's easy with some minor roads in the early stages and you discover idyllic villages built in mellow red sandstone. Historic Kirkoswald with its cobbled market square is first on the list followed a few miles further on by Croglin and its Dracula associations. A series of villages and hamlets follow, strung out at the foot of the Pennine range with their backs firmly set against the prevailing winds. The day ends in picturesque Melmerby with its huge village greens surrounded by warm sandstone buildings and backed by an impressive limestone scar. As much of the walk is over farmland, including fields used for lambing, care must be taken especially during April and early May, particularly in relation to dogs.

Lazonby at the start of the walk is a village which straddles the main street, with the Settle to Carlisle railway bisecting it at right angles. The village was in existence by 1165, its population increasing with the coming of the railway. Thousands of workers, known as 'navvies' came to work in the Eden valley in the late nineteenth century. The construction of the railway was no easy task, it took seven years with only muscle power and dynamite to lay seventy-two miles of tracks. Twenty major viaducts had to be built and fourteen tunnels constructed through some of the harshest landscape in England. The living was hard and drinking and fighting were commonplace, so much so that the Midland Railway Company felt obliged to introduce missionaries to help subdue the worst excesses of the workers. The line ran from Settle in the Yorkshire Dales to Carlisle in Cumbria and was built to link the area with the industrial centres of the Midlands. It proved very popular with the Victorians and was advertised as 'the most picturesque route to Scotland'. The line was scheduled for closure in 1983 but so fierce was the opposition that it was given a reprieve. Over the intervening years the local authorities and various groups have worked closely with British Rail to repair the line and open up some of the smaller stations including that at Lazonby.

Many of the village buildings are of pink tinted Permian sandstone which is common in the Eden valley. This warm, mellowing stone is delightful to look at particularly when the sun's rays fall on it and it blends in so well with the landscape. Unfortunately it is extremely soft and soon crumbles and flakes. To combat this the villagers paint the sills and jambs. Buff, chocolate and maroon used to be the most favoured colours, however modern times call for brighter colours and now jonquil and narvik blue are more popular. Lazonby had its own quarry which produced a much better quality stone but at a price too high for the cottagers. Only the more wealthy folk could afford to build their fine halls with it.

The Parish Church of St Nicholas was built in 1863 and designed by Anthony Salvin. On a mound in the churchyard stands an impressive red sandstone Celtic cross. The inscription at its base reads: BY THY CROSS AND PASSION GOOD LORD DELIVER US. There are stunning views from here, down to the River Eden and beyond. The Eden Bridge may just be glimpsed through the trees, with Kirkoswald, which is your first port of call, in the distance.

Lazonby's main claim to fame is as the 'foremost greyfaced lamb centre'. The annual sheep sales in late summer and autumn are huge affairs with upwards of 16,000 lambs changing hands. The greyfaced lamb is a cross between the Swaledale ewe and the blue-faced Leicester tup and has a curly fleece and speckled head and feet.

Leave Lazonby with the parish church on your left, which is just downhill from the railway station. Turn left immediately after the parish church signed to Armathwaite and Baronwood. You will pass the auction mart on your left before leaving all the houses of Lazonby behind. As you walk along this quiet lane Kirkoswald can be seen over to your right on the hillside. Soon the road drops down over Dyer's Beck and when it starts to rise you'll see a stone stile on your right. Go over here and follow the fence on your left until you reach the beck. Cross over here and keep straight on in the same direction towards Eden Bridge, leaving the fence and beck which have swung away left. When you reach a fence at the far side of the field, turn left in front of it until you reach a stile in it. Once over here cross the next field towards a dry stone wall ahead. Go over the stile here to reach the Eden road bridge at GR 550404.

Turn left here and follow the road over the River Eden. The bridge is a beautiful four-arched, red sandstone bridge, so typical of many

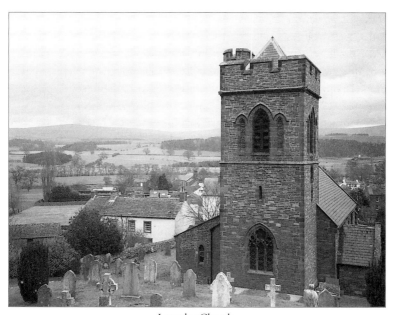

Lazonby Church.

Kirkoswald Church.

which cross the Eden on its long journey from the high bleak moorland of Mallerstang through the lush Eden valley to the sea on the
Solway Firth. Follow the road for one kilometre to reach the village
of Kirkoswald.

As you approach the village, the Parish Church of St Oswald can be
seen over to your right at the base of a hill, with its bell tower up on
the hill behind. Its unusual position some distance from the church
was possibly to help the villagers of Kirkoswald to more readily hear
the church bells. This is the only example of a campanile in old
Cumberland and was built in 1893 in memory of John Henry Ransome
who was the vicar from 1877 to 1892. It replaced an earlier wooden
structure of 1747.

The Norman church is dedicated to St Oswald, King of North-
umbria. In the seventh century the local pagans worshipped at a well
here. However, with the advent of Christianity, this was superseded
by a wooden church, and in 1130 its wooden structure was replaced
by a stone one. In the sixteenth century alterations resulted in the
church we see today, apart from some strengthening of the foundations. This was done in 1970 when it was discovered that the original
foundations were of oak piles. At the church entrance is a magnificent
wooden porch, surviving from about 1523. Inside are twelfth-century
aisles and the base of a chancel arch dating from the same period.
There's also some beautiful stained glass depicting, amongst other
things, the coats of arms of the Featherstonhaughs – the prominent

local family. Outside on the west side of the church is a well dedicated to St Oswald and into which fresh springwater flows. Above the well is the following inscription:-

> To the greater glory of God
> and in honour of
> OSWALD
> King of Northumbria 634 – 642 AD
> Patron of this church
> This tablet was placed over
> ST OSWALD'S WELL
> 'For with thee is the well of life
> and in thy light shall we see light'
>
> Psalm XXXVI. 9.

A metal cup on a long chain enables the visitor to sample the spring water – it really is quite refreshing! Around the church walls either side of the porch are Norman and Saxon grave lids and head stones containing beautiful carvings.

On the embankment beside the church path is a cross made from daffodil bulbs which must look quite impressive when all the flowers are in bloom. The path leading to the church and flanked by an avenue of limes, was used by priests over 400 years ago on their way from the college which is on the left side of the road but not visible. The seventeenth-century entrance to the college is rather impressive and leads to the private residence of the Fetherstonhaugh family who have lived there since the sixteenth century.

A college of priests was founded in 1523, based in a fifteenth-century pele tower which was built originally as a defence against the border raids. The grounds which slope down to the river were converted into herb and kitchen gardens for the priests and a bowling green was also included. The college had a brief life as it was dissolved after only 24 years at Henry VIII's instigation. The Fetherstonhaugh family bought the college and lands in the late sixteenth century and extended the buildings over subsequent generations.

At the crossroads on reaching Kirkoswald, follow the road round to the left. The road straight ahead leads to Kirkoswald Castle which is now in ruins and on private land. Go over Raven Beck, to reach the

Kirkoswald.

village shop and post office on your right. Your route lies along the first road off to your right and signed to Park Head and High Bankhill, but you may wish to walk on a few metres to the cobbled village square.

The Black Bull on the right hand side is a Kirkoswald pub with no beer! The building has been a private house for some time but unfortunately the owners are not allowed to take the pub sign down because of its 'heritage' status. The poor occupants are disturbed continually during the summer months by people walking in and asking for a pint! The village, which is named after St Oswald, boasts some fine early eighteenth-century houses built in the local sandstone. King John granted Kirkoswald a charter in 1201 when it became a busy trading centre, with sheep sales on a grand scale. The castle was built by Randolph Engayn circa 1200 and was improved and extended by subsequent owners. It was reputed to be one of the finest halls in the north of England, with many towers and chapels containing panelling and beautiful stained glass. Little remains apart from a tower and the remnants of a spiral staircase.

Kirkoswald's position on the banks of the Raven Beck meant that water played a large part in the life of the village. Over the years there have been corn and paper mills, a saw and bobbin mill, one

for carding and spinning and a brewery; however, agriculture is the
main employment today.

As mentioned earlier, your route lies along a road with a footpath
sign to Parkhead, alongside the old bank and across the road from
the Manor House. This was built in 1703 for the mill manager; note
the three painted windows, done to avoid paying window tax. A few
metres along the road are Hazel and Acacia cottages on your left,
built to house estate workers. At the end of the tarmac keep straight
on along a track. On your left along here is the concrete channel
which once carried water from the mill race to the corn mill.

Raven Beck can be glimpsed down the slope to your right as it
forces its way through a mini gorge before going under the bridge.
After the mill race crosses your path, just upstream, are two sluice
gates. One of these channels water over the metal aqueduct to the
sawmill, which you've just passed on your right. Go on through a
wooden gate into a field with a weir on your right. It makes quite a
roar and can be heard before you even reach it. Follow the footpath
beside the river. At the end of the field go through a kissing gate to
enter woodland and in a few metres where the path divides, fork left
uphill. Climb up through the trees, where bluebells, wood anemones
and wild raspberries abound in spring and summer. Bear left at a
waymark and carry on to the top of the woodland. An old seat is

High Bankhill.

positioned near the top if you feel like a rest, although it could be a rather uncomfortable rest. When I was there last there were many brambles growing through the iron seat!

As you emerge from the trees you'll see a stile in the fence on your left. Go over here, turn right and follow the fence on your right until it swings away right. At this point keep on uphill but slightly leftish, aiming to the left of a large tree, eventually to reach a stile in the dry stone wall ahead of you. Once over here follow the obvious path diagonally left towards some houses. Go through a kissing gate and out onto a road at GR 560420. Turn right here and follow the road for 100 metres. At a crossroads turn left, signed to Croglin. After a few metres there's a beautiful thatched cottage on your right dated 1693. Follow the road round to the right and keep on it for some four kilometres (2½ miles) until you reach GR557458. (Fortunately there's a wide grass verge for most of its length.)

At the first crossroads, ignore the main road which swings away right, signed to Croglin and keep straight on along a minor road towards Grindledyke. Soon Grindledyke Farm comes into view with Wind Fell to the right of it. This minor road is quiet enough and it gives you the opportunity to experience the tranquil atmosphere and beauty of the Eden valley. The scene is one of lush green pasture land and gently rolling hills. The fields are bounded by dry stone walls all built in the local red sandstone and encrusted with emerald green mosses and soft grey lichens. As you reach the highest point on the road, just past the farm, fabulous views unfold of the Pennine range over to your right with the Lakeland fells behind you. As the road drops down towards Croglin Water you may care to ponder on the legend of the Croglin Bat.

Croglin Low Hall, which you will reach soon, is the scene of this famous legend and thought to be the inspiration for Bram Stoker's 'Dracula'. Amelia Cranswell and her two brothers were staying at Croglin Low Hall in 1875. During the night Amelia was attacked by a cloaked demon who savagely bit her throat and neck. The demon escaped across the fells, leaving Amelia alive but badly bitten. Later that year the demon bat appeared again at Amelia's window but this time her brothers were waiting. They chased it across the fields to Croglin cemetery where it disappeared into a vault. When the vault was opened the following day it was discovered that all the coffins had been smashed – save one. Inside this lay the semi-decomposed body of a cloaked man with fresh blood dripping from his fangs.

Edward Cranswell drove a stake through the demon's heart and the villagers set the coffin and its contents on fire in the churchyard. Amelia's bedroom was closed up and the window remains bricked up to this day. All this happened approximately 20 years before Bram Stoker's book was published.

Ignore a road off to the right at GR557445 which goes to Renwick and keep straight on towards Croglin Low Hall. Quite soon the farm buildings can be seen over to your left. After approximately one kilometre you reach a farm track on your right to Croglin High Hall (just before the bridge over Croglin Water). Turn right here and follow the farm track until you're about half-way along. Go over a stile on your left and aim for a telegraph pole which is waymarked. Keep straight on beside the remains of an old fence, passing a further telegraph pole. Keep to the high ground until you join a fence coming in from the right. Go over a makeshift stile in the fence, turn left and follow the fence uphill to go through an old gateway. Keep climbing until you reach a gate. Once through here turn immediately right and go over a fence. Turn immediately left and follow the fence until it goes slightly left, keep straight on here towards a gate ahead. Go over the stile to the right of the gate and keep straight on, following a dry stone wall on your left. At the end of the field go through the gate ahead and follow a fence on your left all the way to Caber Farm.

Go through the farmyard, passing the farmhouse on your right and turn immediately left through a gate. Follow a track between stone walls, through a further gate ahead and keep straight on, passing a farm shed on your left. Go through another gate and keep straight on with a fence on your left. Pass through a gate at the end of the field and go diagonally left to reach a dry stone wall. Keep on in the same direction. There are delightful views of Croglin Water in the valley bottom as it makes its way down from high up on Scarrow-manwick Fell (what an incredibly spooky name for a fell – the imagination runs riot!). This was also the route taken by the Croglin Bat on its way to the vault in Croglin church yard. On a more factual note, the banks of Croglin Water are notorious for big black midges which emerge in stinging hordes at dusk. The results of their bites may be not too dissimilar from that of a vampire, you have been warned! On a more cheerful note, there's a delightful picnic spot beside the river, just before you reach the road. Follow the obvious path through a series of gates to reach the road at GR576467. If you've plenty of time a left turn here will bring you after 500 metres to Croglin village and a pub.

The Robin Hood is only open at lunchtimes on Friday, Saturday and Sunday. Croglin Church dates from 1878 and has neo-Norman windows and a double bellcote. Directly opposite lies a fifteenth-century pele tower which originally housed the church rector.

Otherwise turn right and follow the road for 300 metres as it climbs. Soon you'll see a gate and a sign on your left to Scale Houses and Busk. Turn through here on a good track and follow a fence on your left to reach a gate which takes you into the wood. Follow the waymarks through the wood with Lino Beck on your right. Some pheasant pens can be seen on your left. At the time of writing a full size female dummy, dressed in army combat gear, was leaning up against one of the pens. This unexpected apparition sent my blood pressure into orbit! When the track swings away left, keep straight on, following the line of the beck along a lovely mossy path. You are now in the middle of a copse of pine trees with only the occasional birdsong and the trickle of the beck to break the stillness all around you.

As you emerge from the forest, cross over the beck and go over a stile ahead, followed immediately by another. Make your way back over the beck and, following the line of the beck, climb the hillside. Make your way towards the buildings at Davygill. Go through a gate and, passing the buildings on your right, go through a further gate ahead to enter a walled lane. Go through another gateway and as the track curves away left uphill, keep straight on with a wall on your right. Follow this other track until you reach a rocky knoll on the right and a further gate beside it, (ignore a gate on your right). Go through here and keep on along the obvious track, crossing over Lino Beck again, and eventually you reach a gate which takes you out into a walled lane at GR586458. This track is known as Clint Lane and leads up to a disused mine high on Scarrowmanick Fell. Turn right along here and enjoy the superb views as you start to drop downhill. Shortly you reach a gated stile in the wall on your left. Go through here and keep straight on up the field with a wall over to your right. Just before you reach the far end of the field you'll see another gated stile in the wall on your right. Once through here walk diagonally left to reach a gate in the wall ahead of you. Go through the gate, over the track and over a stile in the wall ahead.

Cross the field, making your way diagonally towards a wall on your right. Follow the wall along and soon the buildings of Scale Houses come into view. Go over a gate/stile in the far corner of the field and follow a wall on your right. Eventually you reach another gate in the far corner of the field which takes you out onto the road. Turn right here through the hamlet of Scale Houses and at a crossroads turn left and follow a sign to Renwick and Busk.

These tiny hamlets and villages lie at the base of the Pennine fellsides like a string of pearls beneath the fells, each one a jewel in its own right. It is so easy to imagine how life used to be at the beginning of the century as you walk through these hamlets, so little has changed in the intervening years. Their houses are solid structures built with their backs to the east in defence against the dreaded Helm Wind, the only wind in England to have its own name. Its power can be tremendous when it sweeps down the escarpment from Cross Fell, wreaking havoc as it goes. The Helm Wind has been known to blow for nine days at a time and is most frequent in late winter and spring.

Follow a good track and when it starts to descend you'll pass a stile in the fence on your left. Ignore this! and keep straight on until you reach four gates, two either side of the track. Go through the second gate on your right and walk diagonally across the field, over a hump in the middle before dropping down towards a stile in the wall ahead of you. Keep on in the same direction towards the far corner of the field set amongst a little group of trees. Go over the stile here towards a dry stone wall a few yards ahead of you, turn left and walk along this keeping the wall/fence on your right. Soon you reach another stile in the wall on your right, go through here and head towards the village of Renwick which is in the distance. Go through a gateway and keep straight on to reach the corner of a wall and a track coming in from the left, turn right along here to reach the road. Turn left along the road and follow it to Renwick.

As you enter the village look out for two unusual figures on your left, atop the gateposts at the entrance to The Rookeries. This is immediately before the Church of All Saints which was the scene of yet another gruesome legend. The ancient church had fallen into disrepair and was demolished. The villagers gathered together amongst the ruins to help with the rebuilding process. Suddenly a monstrous animal with the body of a cock and the tail of a serpent flew up from the rubble. Most of the villagers fled but one John Tallentyre stayed to do battle with the cockatrice. Grasping a branch from a rowan

Gatepost figures at the
Rookeries, Renwick.

tree (said to ward off witches) he beat the animal to death. Other
versions of the story talk of a 'monstrous bat'. Whatever, with all this
talk of vampires perhaps you should carry a few cloves of garlic around
your neck just to be on the safe side.

Shortly after the church is a Methodist Chapel on your right,
followed by two semi-derelict buildings which were originally an
eighteenth-century coaching inn. A driveway leads through an arch
to where stables used to be at the back. In the nineteenth century
the village was a bustling community with at least four pubs and
several blacksmiths. Apart from mills which were powered by the
local becks, there was a thriving coal industry, the mines being high
up on Thackmoor and Renwick Fell; the tracks can still be found
leading out of the village and up onto the fells. During the packhorse
era horses pulled the coal carts both to Kirkoswald market and also
over the wild Pennine moors to the valley of the South Tyne, hence
the reason for so many blacksmiths.

Keep straight on through the village past the road which swings right
to Kirkoswald and Alston. Take the right fork in the road, just after

the phone box, and follow it to a walled lane, signed to Raven Bridge. Soon you need to pass through two sets of gates to the right of some farm buildings. Drop down here with a concrete wall on your left towards a wood. Keep low down, ignoring a track which goes up left to the wood, and make your way towards another copse of trees. Go through a gate ahead of you with How Wood on your left and follow the fence beside the wood until it turns slightly left. Keep straight on here to cut the corner off and eventually reach the road at the far side of the field.

HERE A DECISION HAS TO BE MADE.

The route here goes immediately left through a gate signposted to Outhwaite and Haresceugh where, after a kilometre of walking, stepping stones are reached over Raven Beck. In good weather there should be no problem; however after heavy rain in autumn and winter the stepping stones can be submerged, making a crossing of the river rather difficult. If this is the case it might be better to carry on along the road to Haresceugh where you can rejoin the route.

ALTERNATIVE:

If the road is your choice, turn left here and follow the road all the way to the hamlet of Haresceugh. Ignore the road off to your right soon after the bridge and signed to Unthank. You might care to stop and look for a milestone low down on your left just beyond the road bridge. Part of the inscription has been obliterated but it relates to the Manor of Haresceugh and the words 'Boundary Perambulation' are visible.

These stones were visited each year on Rogation Sunday, or on any of the three following days, by as many of the villagers as possible. The Rogation rituals are very old and the original object of the procession was to ask for God's blessing upon the New Year's crops. The perambulation was useful at a time when maps were scarce as a simple means of determining and remembering where the parish limits ran. Young people were often bumped upon the actual boundary stones, thrown into streams or ponds which formed the boundary, dragged through hedges or forced to climb over roofs of houses which were built across the boundary line. They were rewarded for their pains with money or gifts. The idea was that they should never forget

Raven Beck stepping stones.

where the actual boundary markers lay should a dispute arise in the future – not much chance of that!

OTHERWISE, as mentioned previously, turn left through the gate and follow the path which climbs up through the trees until you reach a gate. Once through here keep on along the obvious path with a wall on your left and Raven Beck over to your right. Follow the main path as it eventually climbs the hillside and, at a point where it turns sharp left to go up to Outhwaite, drop down diagonally right to reach a fence. Turn right along it and drop down the steep bank and continue down the field to reach Raven Beck, where a stile will take you to the stepping stones.

At the other side of the beck cross the stile into the woodland. Follow the track up through the wood, continue up the path and cross the stile at the top. Turn immediately right along the fence, then turn left to walk straight ahead up the hill, with the wall on your right. Hartside Pass is visible ahead on the Pennine fellside. At 580 metres above sea level, this is the high point on a road which strikes over the fells to Alston. At this high point is a cafe which is open in the summer months and is visible on the skyline. It enters the record books as the highest cafe in England. The views from Hartside Pass are magnificent, taking in the lush Eden valley nestling between the Pennine escarpment and the mountains of the Lake District. At the brow of the hill bear left to the corner of the small paddock and then to the gate out onto the road. Turn right towards Haresceugh.

At the hamlet, where the road swings right, is a gate on your left and a sign to Busk at GR 610429. THIS IS WHERE YOU MEET UP WITH THE ALTERNATIVE ROUTE ALONG THE ROAD FROM RAVEN BRIDGE AND IT IS ALSO YOUR ROUTE OUT OF THE HAMLET.

Spare a few moments though to take a look at Haresceugh. It is difficult to imagine it now but this tiny hamlet was once quite a busy place. It stood on the medieval Via Regia or Monarch's Highway, being the route used by the king as he travelled around his kingdom. Note the farm on your left with its exterior stone steps, so typical of the buildings in the area. There are those who still remember cows being milked in the open here with the farmer seated on the traditional three-legged stool. The cottage opposite once housed a pub.

Make your way back to the Busk sign. Go through the gate here and drop down on a good track, over a little beck and up to the ruins of Haresceugh Castle.

Little remains now, but this was once one of many castles which guarded the Monarch's Highway. The 'luck of Haresceugh Castle' relates to a 20-centimetre-diameter bowl which has unfortunately disappeared. On its silver rim was an inscription:

'Should this bowl fall in feast or wassail
Farewell the luck of Haresceugh Castle'

Legend also has it that a secret tunnel existed between the castle and Kirkoswald and also that a pot full of guineas lies hidden in the cellars beneath the ruins. If only you'd brought that metal detector along with you!

Carry on along the track, through a gate ahead and drop down the field with a wall on your right to reach Lonning Lane. The mast over to your left beneath Fiend's Fell is owned by British Telecom and to my mind appears totally out of place in such a dramatic landscape. There is a direct route to Busk from Lonning Lane which was obstructed at the time of writing. If there's a waymarked stile on the other side of the lane, go over here and follow the waymarked route all the way to the hamlet. Otherwise turn right along Lonning Lane and follow it round to the left, passing a plantation on the same side. At the end of the trees is a gate, turn through here and follow the farm track beside the plantation. At the end of the trees go diagonally right towards the hamlet of Busk. When you reach a gateway in a semi-derelict enclosure, go through here and keep straight on to pass through another gate at the far end. Go through here and turn right to pass immediately through another gateway. Pass through a final gateway, signed to Fellgate. Follow the tarmac road through the hamlet of Busk.

These remote hamlets and villages were considered to be the last habitable places before reaching the wild moorland beyond. No doubt the miners living another 300 metres higher up in a 'mine shop' on Melmerby Fell though so too. Their living conditions were primitive to say the least, their only consolation being the thought of trekking home at the weekends to their families lower down the valleys.

After passing the last of the buildings in the hamlet, at a point where the road swings away right, go straight on through a gate signed to Cannerheugh. Follow the track past the farm buildings, going through two sets of gates. At the third gate (where the track ends and you enter an open field) turn right along the side of a dry stone wall. Ignore the two gates in the bottom corner of the field and turn left along the wall until you reach a further gate. Go through here and go diagonally right across the field towards a telegraph pole until you reach a stile in the wall ahead. Once over here cross over the farm track and keep straight on just to the left of the same telegraph pole to reach another stile in the wall ahead. Go over here and carry on in the same direction towards Eller Beck which is flanked by a line of trees. Go over the stile and bridge here and follow a wall which is at right-angles to the beck, along its left side. Keep straight on with the wall on your right until you enter what was once an old track. Follow this as it swings right through a gateway and a few metres further along a further gate takes you out onto the road at GR608409. Turn left here and follow the road towards Unthank. When the road forks, take the right one which takes you through the village. As you walk along this tiny road you can take in the wonderful views of the Lakeland fells in the distance to your right.

Where the road turns left, go right (signed to Gamblesby) and walk past the first building on your left. Take the track off to the left straight after this building and directly before a gate across your path. Follow the track down to a gate, once through here go over a little beck and keep straight on up the track with a fence on your right, soon going over a track which crosses your path. Go through a gate ahead with a wall on your right and follow the wall as it swings round to the right. Soon you'll reach a gate in the wall, (unfortunately the stile just beyond it was blocked at the time of writing) go through here and turn left following the wall until it swings away left. Leave it here and keep straight on towards some houses. Go through a kissing gate beside a house and follow a hedged path to reach the road. In early spring this tiny path is smothered in a carpet of delicate white snowdrops, epitomising for me the rebirth of the year. Turn right along the road to reach Gamblesby village.

As the road starts to drop down a little, just before the Glassonby turn off on the right is a raised embankment on your left with some old barns above it. Set into the wall of one of the barns is a plaque

Unthank.

dedicated to John Wesley. The inscription is as follows: 'John Wesley preached on this hill 1751 & 1780'.

John Wesley was the chief evangelist of the Methodist Revival movement. This movement gained in popularity in the Pennines area in the eighteenth century alongside an increase in population which was largely due to the rapid growth of the lead mining industry. Wesley was an energetic man who travelled widely to spread his gospel. He held great appeal for the miners who could relate to a preacher who shared their own background which was in stark contrast to the wealth of the Church of England and its ministers.

As you pass that Glassonby turn off, take note of the old stocks which are on the other side of the road on top of a stepped platform. They are unusual in that they are made of iron instead of wood and are padlocked. There is a village shop cum Post Office in the village which is open every day and only closes at lunchtime on Monday, Thursday and Sunday. It is just beyond the Red Lion pub on the other side of the road.

Go past an old church on your right followed by the Red Lion pub on your left. After the next house beyond the pub is a gateway on the left, go through here. (If you reach the post box in the wall on your left, you've gone too far.) Follow this good farm track until you reach a gate on your left and a turning on your right, go right here and keep on until you reach a staggered crossroads. Go right at this point and shortly you reach a ford. Once you've negotiated this then carry on all the way to Melmerby, almost two kilometres (1¼ miles) distant.

Up to your left above the woods is Melmerby Scar. The limestone from here was famous for its light colour, free from impurities and was burnt in the local lime kilns. The lime was used as a sweetener, turning the acidic fellside into ground suitable for grazing animals on. Beyond Melmerby Scar lies the bulk of Cross Fell. This is the highest point of the whole Pennine range at 893 metres and has the Pennine Way Long Distance Footpath going over its summit. Legend has it that its original name was Fiend's Fell. This was changed to Cross Fell after a cross had been erected in an attempt to convert the local Celts to Christianity. This impressive top has a large summit plateau from where views of Scotland can be had on a clear day (not that there are too many of these as Cross Fell is not noted for its

good weather!). The remains of a sheepfold provide shelter for the
many walkers who visit the summit. An ambition of mine is one day
to watch the sun rise from here. There are some who say that you've
never lived till you've seen the dawn from Cross Fell. Maybe this will
be my year.

> At the road at GR615377 turn left and keep on to reach your desti-
> nation at Melmerby. Just as you enter the village you'll pass one of
> the old AA signs on the gable end of an old barn, with the helpful
> information that London is only 297½ miles away. Opposite is the
> Melmerby Caravan Park on your right.

Melmerby is an absolute gem, nestling beneath the bleak Pennine
fells. Its large 13-acre green is surrounded by warm sandstone buildings,
built close together in protection against the dreaded Helm Wind
and the equally dreaded border raiders – not that there are many
raiders around today. Melmerby Hall was built round an existing
defensive tower, the main buildings are Georgian with seventeenth-
and eighteenth-century additions. The old Wesleyan chapel and
former school are now private dwellings but the church-like tower of
the old school is unmistakable. The shop and Post Office, on the left

Melmerby.

as you enter the village, were once an inn. Fortunately for us the Shepherds Inn beyond still dispenses ale as well as excellent food.

Prior to the last century Melmerby was famous for its mid-summer fire festival. These festivals had their origins back in pagan times and the fires were often lit to drive out evil and bring fertility and prosperity. The 'Melmerby Rounds' attracted people from far and wide, when running races were held along with cock fighting, hound trailing and Cumberland wrestling. It is said that the wrestling ring was paved with sheep's knuckle bones!

Melmerby is more recently famous for its award-winning bakery. Housed in a converted stone barn beside the green, the bakery sells superb bread and cakes cooked using traditional methods in wood-fired brick ovens. The restaurant serves food every day, much of the ingredients for which are organically grown on the five-acre holding behind the bakery. A well-stocked shop, complete with organic wines and preserves, completes the picture.

The village has several B&Bs, the Shepherds Inn serves food but has no accommodation, and the Post Office houses a cafe. In summer the Isis Gallery can also be visited. It specialises in contemporary Northern artists.

Walk 4

Day two
Melmerby to Lazonby

Distance 14.4 kms (9 miles)
Ordnance Survey Map
1:25,000
    Pathfinder 568 – Southwaite & Kirkoswald (Cumbria)
    (tiny pt.)
    Pathfinder 577 – Penrith (North)
    Pathfinder 578 – Appleby-in-Westmorland
1:50,000
    Landranger 86 – Haltwhistle, Bewcastle & Alston area
    (tiny pt.)
    Landranger 90 – Penrith & Keswick
    Landranger 91 – Appleby

*T*here is easy walking again through farmland with some minor roads in the early stages. Expansive views are enjoyed almost all the way to the incredible pre-historic monument of Long Meg and her daughters. Sadly the pub in Little Salkeld closed some time ago but there's a tea room which may be open at the watermill and guided tours are available on certain days. The latter half of the walk follows the course of the River Eden with impressive views of the Long Meg viaduct before Lacy's Caves are reached. These marvellous caves cut out of the rock are another highlight of the walk. There then follows a delightful walk beside the mighty Eden before reaching journey's end at Lazonby.

Leave Melmerby along the A686 Langwathby road and follow it for approximately one kilometre with a wood on your right. Where the

The old school, Melmerby.

wood ends at GR608374 you reach a gate and a footpath sign on your right. Go through the gate and follow a track with the wood beside you. Do not go through the gate which shortly crosses your path but turn left and follow a wall to the end of the field. Go through a gateway here and keep on to pass Birknab Wood. Go through another gate at the end of the wood side, followed by a further gate, to reach a road. Keep straight on along the road, going due west and ignoring a farm road which you soon reach off to the left to Melmerby Mill. Follow the road over a beck and passing Broadmeadows Farm on your right. Immediately after this you reach a gate on your left. Go through here and walk diagonally right across the field towards a telegraph pole. Just to the right of this is a further gate, go through here, turn right and follow a fence and hedge on your right.

At the far end of the field, just to the left of the corner is a stile in the fence, go over here and keep on in the same direction with a fence on your right. When you reach the corner of the fence just prior to the farm buildings at Farmanby, make your way over a wire to join a track going to the farm. At the farm go through the gate ahead and straight on through the farm yard. Follow the track round, passing the farmhouse on your right, and keep on along the track all the way to the road at GR588368.

Turn right along the road and follow it for almost two kilometres (1¼ miles). This minor road has a broad grass verge for most of its length and provides good fast walking with excellent views all around. Ignore the road which you shortly reach off to the left to Penrith and keep on all the way to an old school adjacent to some crossroads.

The impressive Pennine chain of hills is your companion on the right whilst the Lakeland hills are over to your left. The lush arable land of the Eden Valley is sheltered between these two ranges. The valley is virtually unspoilt and is bypassed by many on their rush to reach the Lakeland hills. However the area is gaining in popularity, particularly with walkers. There are several long distance paths which pass through the valley including the Eden Way and Lady Anne's Way.

Keep straight on at the crossroads, following the sign to Glassonby. After passing a copse of trees on your right (just before the Glassonby road sign) is a road on your left to Maughanby Farm. Turn along here and after approximately 400 metres you reach a gate on either side of the track (ignore a more haphazard arrangement of gates 100 metres before this). The gate on the right leads to St Michael's Church, confusingly known as Addingham church, whilst the one on the left is your route to Long Meg.

The church is well worth a visit, dating from about the sixteenth century and with external bells of a century earlier. Addingham church and village, which were situated on the banks of the Eden near Daleraven, were washed away in 1160 by floods. A collection of carved stones from that church can be found here in St Michael's Church porch.

A particular curiosity is that inside the church can be seen the base of a large stone cross marked with the lines for the ancient game of Nine Men's Morris – also known as trios, merrils, ninepenny morals and, in the Isle of Wight, 'siege of Troy'. Evidence of this once-popular game crops up throughout the country and can be found wherever people congregated – carved on tables or seats, cut in turf, scratched on floors and windowsills, as well as more formally on specially-made boards with holes drilled to receive the pegs with which the game was played. The object was to get three of your pegs, stones or counters in a row on the intersections of the lines or

The 'Hammer-head'
cross in Glassonby
Church yard

the three angles of one corner with the two players taking it in turns.
The game's layout suggests a link with ancient labyrinths or mazes
as well as the children's game of hopscotch. In the churchyard, on
your left as you approach the church porch, is an old weather beaten
'hammer-head' cross, possibly eleventh-century.

If not visiting the church, turn left here through the gate (which is
waymarked) and keep straight on, following a wall on your right until
you reach a copse of trees. Go through a gate to the right of the
plantation and follow the obvious path. Long Meg and her daughters
can clearly be seen ahead of you. The most prominent stone is of
course Long Meg herself. At the edge of the plantation go through a
gate and keep on with a wall on your right to the end of the field.
Go through another gate and follow a hedge and fence on your left
to the end of the next field. Pass through another gate to reach the
field containing Long Meg and her daughters – definitely the highlight
of the walk.

This Neolithic stone circle is one of the largest in the country at one
hundred metres or so in diameter – and yet it is relatively unknown
in relation to its cousins in the south, Stonehenge and Avebury. The
tallest stone, Long Meg, is made of Penrith sandstone while her

'daughters' are of a flinty limestone. Positioned directly in front of her are four stones in a square formation. The total number of stones in the circle is a matter of conjecture as every book I've read gives a different figure – anything from sixty-six to eighty! (It's said that anyone who manages to count the same number of stones twice will either incur the wrath of the devil or else Long Meg herself will come to life. Don't say I didn't warn you!)

Myths and legends abound; one has it that Long Meg and her daughters were witches who were turned to stone for dancing on the Sabbath, another insists that Meg will bleed if the stone is chipped or broken. Certainly any efforts in the past to destroy the stones seem to have been thwarted in one way or another. In 1725 Colonel Lacy of Salkeld Hall, tried to blow up the stones in order to use them as milestones. As the work commenced a tremendous storm blew up and the workmen fled for their lives, convinced that the Druids had come to wreak vengeance on them for desecrating their holy temple. Colonel Lacy gave up the task, for which we are extremely grateful, and built his own remarkable monument in the form of Lacy's caves which you will see later.

On the side of Long Meg facing the circle can be seen cup and ring symbols which are expressive of ancient notions of rebirth and she is sited so that her four angles coincide with the four points of the compass. If you sit in the centre of the circle on an evening in midwinter you will see the sun set directly over Long Meg, signalling the turning of the year and suggesting the circle was intended as a clock or calendar. Maybe this was also the reason for Meg's great height or possibly it was so that she could act as a signpost for travellers to the site. She can certainly be seen for some distance. It is sobering to consider that this circle was positioned here before the Egyptian pyramids were built and its existence points not only to the great organisational and technological ability of our ancestors, but also to their understanding of the planets and stars, the earth and the sun – and probably much that we have long since lost. Whatever the driving force behind its construction, it certainly must have been a very powerful one when you realise that the only tools available were of flint, stone and bone.

If you stand with your back to Meg and her daughters you can enjoy far reaching views along the Eden valley. Cross Fell is clearly visible, diagonally right, with the 'pikes' of Knock, Dufton and Murton strung out beside her. Further right are the Lakeland Fells, while the Howgills lie in the far distance ahead of you. Altogether a superb spot to be on a clear day with magnificent scenery all around you and ancient history (or is it prehistory?) at your feet. Well, if you've finished counting the stones it's time to be off.

Leave the field by the tarmac road and follow it downhill towards Little Salkeld. You are now dropping back down into the lush green pastures of the Eden Valley, leaving the remote East Fellside behind. At a point where the road swings away left, keep straight on along a track and then turn right when you eventually reach the road. As you drop down the road here, the second group of buildings you pass on the left, set back from the road, was once a pub known as the Druids Head. Bad news for those of us who like a pint at this stage of a walk.

Where the road bends left in the village, signed to Penrith, keep straight on. That is unless you need a cup of tea. Just 200 metres down that road is Little Salkeld Mill with its accompanying tea-room (only open Monday, Tuesday and Thursday between March and October, though).

The watermill is one of the few left in the country which still produces stoneground flours using traditional waterpower. The eighteenth-century mill uses two 12ft-diameter overshot waterwheels which power two millstones, each weighing half a ton.

Keep straight on once more, passing a lovely red sandstone building on your right with an enormous ship's bell outside. After passing Townend Farm on your right continue on the farm road as it curves right, signed to Lacy's Caves. The Settle to Carlisle Railway line can now be seen over to your left. The line was opened in 1876 and even Little Salkeld had its own railway station.

Part way up the hillside beyond the railway and river is Great Salkeld. The two villages were linked at one time by a bridge over the Eden, but this was washed away in a great flood in 1360. St Cuthbert's Church in Great Salkeld boasts an impressive fortified tower which is clearly visible. This battlemented tower was built in the fourteenth century as a refuge for the villagers during the infamous border raids.

For the rest of your journey you follow the course of the River Eden all the way back to Lazonby. From this elevated position there are beautiful views of the broad river wending its way along the valley floor, backed by patterned fields which rise up on the far side. Eventually you come to a ruined building on your right known as Throstle Hall and dated 1880. It was originally two cottages and an engine house and had some connection with the nearby Long Meg Mine which was a major source of gypsum and anhydrite in the late nineteenth century. The gypsum was used for plaster of Paris and the anhydrite for sulphuric acid. Shortly after the ruin the entrance to Long Meg mine is reached. Turn left here, following a sign to Lacy's Caves (and passing an electricity sub station on the left), and then turn left again. It is all waymarked and fenced and directs you around Long Meg Sidings.

These extensive sidings were constructed in 1954 to transport the anhydrite to a works in Widnes. Most of the buildings were demolished in 1977 and nature is gradually reclaiming its own. The Settle to Carlisle railway line on your left goes into a cutting at this point and was the scene of a tragic accident in 1918. Engine No. 1010 was hauling an express from St Pancras to Glasgow when it ran into a landslide in the cutting and seven people were killed. In 1933 the same engine

Long Meg viaduct.

Force Mill.

was *en route* to St Pancras when it collided with a goods train, killing the driver. Enginemen forever after feared working the jinxed engine.

Soon the Long Meg viaduct can be glimpsed through the trees. This magnificent structure took four years to build. It stands 18 metres high and needs four of its seven piers permanently in the water. Follow the obvious path along the course of an old branch line which led to the mine. Soon you pass the remains of a shored up wall on your right. This was built to prevent the bank slipping onto the railway line. The line of an old tramway can also be seen climbing up the hillside.

Over to your left, just beyond a couple of metres of wooden fence, is the spot where a bridge once spanned the Eden. (It is possible to scramble down an unofficial path to gain a magnificent view of Force Mill and the weir.) Some of the masonry from the old bridge can still be seen on the near bank. This was a very important river crossing in medieval times. Force Mill on the opposite bank made use of the Eden water to power its machinery as did the mine on this side.

Just a little further on are the ruins on your right of an old Victorian plaster works. The path now drops down to the river side with delightful views along it. Carry on through Cave Wood. The path here is an ancient one used by the miners on their way to the mine from Kirkoswald. Soon Lacy's Caves appear ahead, unmistakeable in their strong red sandstone colouring. As you approach them the main path goes uphill to the right but I would recommend the very short diversion left to visit the caves. I have a lasting impression of vivid warm red sandstone arches, dark interiors and fantastic glimpses of the river framed in the arched doorways. Take note of the warning notices outside the caves though as one false move could be your last!

The five interconnecting caves were excavated out of the soft Eden sandstone by order of Colonel Lacy in the eighteenth century. During this period it was the vogue to have grottoes and romantic ruins on your land and the Colonel even employed a hermit to live in the caves to add a bit of authenticity. Another theory concerning the caves is that they were built as wine cellars (I have a vivid image of a very drunk and happy hermit!). Colonel Lacy certainly used to entertain guests here and there's evidence that gardens existed around the caves; rhododendrons, laburnum and other garden plants can be found growing nearby.

Carry on along the path as it makes its way up the hillside above the caves, before dropping down again to the riverside. Follow the obvious

Lacey's Caves.

Eden Bridge.

path to the end of the plantation and keep on in line with the River Eden over a series of stiles. Eventually the path climbs high above the river before dropping down through the trees to reach the road at GR565395. Turn left along the road to go over Daleraven Bridge. Glassonby Beck, which flows underneath here, forms the boundary between Kirkoswald and Glassonby parishes and the old boundary stone can be found by the bridge, directly beneath the footpath sign to Lacey's Caves. As the road starts to climb you reach a gate on the left and a sign to Eden Bridge. Go through here and follow the left edge of the field, following the line of the river. Lazonby is clearly visible ahead now on the far side of the river. Follow the path by the river, going over a stile at the end of the field and onto a farm track coming in from Mains Farm. Keep on beside the river and go through a gate ahead. Carry on beside the river through a further gate and immediately passing over a tiny bridge. Finally Eden Bridge comes into view. At the end of the next field is a gate and stile. Go over here and follow a fence on your right before reaching a final gate and stile which takes you out onto the road. Turn left here and follow the road over the bridge.

At the end of the bridge, turn left to go through a car park. At the far side of this is an information board which you pass to enter a picnic area. In the far corner lies one of the Eden Benchmarks.

These are sculptures commissioned by the East Cumbria Countryside Project to draw attention to the environment and to help promote a more sensitive attitude to its care. Ten sculptures are planned in all, to be sited along the length of the River Eden. Each one is by a different sculptor and will have a dual purpose as a seat. Five are already in position and the rest should be completed by the year 2000. 'Cypher Piece', here by the Eden Bridge, was sculpted by Francis Pelly and provides a perfect spot from which to view the River Eden flowing beneath the sandstone bridge, set in an enchanting landscape. The gap between the two stones echoes the meandering line of the river.

Keep straight on here along a tiny path between the river and the road. This may be too overgrown in the summer months but it's worth a try as it avoids pounding the tarmac. If it gets too bad you can always hop over the wall onto the road. Eventually you come out onto a cleared area adjacent to the village swimming pool. (There's a camp site beyond the pool.) Turn right here to reach the road and follow it uphill to reach the centre of Lazonby.

I hope you've enjoyed your Melmerby Meander. If the weather's good you could always celebrate with a dip in the local swimming pool or, if you prefer your liquid on the inside, there are two pubs in the village. There's also a supermarket and Post Office. The old school

Lazonby.

now houses Croglin Toys, whose ground floor workshop includes a viewing area where you can watch all manner of items being made (only British hardwoods and sustainable Scandinavian pine are used), while upstairs is the shop.

Only two miles away by road, just the other side of Kirkoswald, lie the well known Nunnery Walks, reputedly one of the most beautiful riverside walks in all England! A series of paths through mature woodland lead you past spectacular waterfalls on the River Croglin before reaching the banks of the Eden. The grounds were laid out in 1750 by Henry Aglionby, about the time when the Nunnery was established. This Benedictine convent is now a hotel and also combines a tea-room. A small charge is payable to enjoy the walks.

Date walked   _____

_____

Companions   _____

_____

_____

Weather   _____

Highlight of the walk   _____

_____

_____

_____

Any other memories   _____

_____

_____

WALK NUMBER FIVE – CIRCULAR
'BARNEY'S ROUND'
Barnard Castle – Middleton-in-Teesdale – Barnard Castle

Total distance 37.6 kms (23.5 miles)
Barnard Castle to Middleton-in-Teesdale 19.2 kms (12 miles)
Middleton-in-Teesdale to Barnard Castle 18.4 kms (11.5 miles)

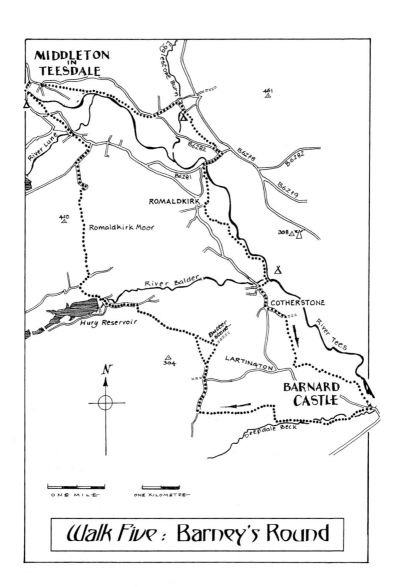

MIDDLETON
IN
TEESDALE

Eggestone Burn

461

River Lune

B6282

B6278

B6282

B6281

B6279

ROMALDKIRK

410

Romaldkirk Moor

308

River Balder

COTHERSTONE

Hury Reservoir

River Tees

Butter Stone

304

LARTINGTON

BARNARD
CASTLE

Deepdale Beck

N

ONE MILE   ONE KILOMETRE

Walk Five : Barney's Round

Walk 5

Day One
Barnard Castle to Middleton-in-Teesdale

Distance 19.2 kms (12 miles)
Ordnance Survey Map
1:25,000
    Outdoor Leisure 31 – Teesdale
1:50,000
    Landranger 92 – Barnard Castle & Richmond

*T*he hustle and bustle of Barnard Castle is left for the remote moors above Baldersdale. We pass through peaceful woodlands before climbing out past the monumental remains of one of the great viaducts of the Victorian railway builders. There follows a lofty walk above Lartington village and over Currack Rigg before dropping down into Baldersdale and on to a scene of tranquil beauty at Hury Reservoir. One more climb takes you up onto Romaldkirk Moor which, because of its elevated position, offers expansive views all around. The day ends with an easy stroll along a disused railway line beside the wild flower meadows which are so typical of Teesdale. There is nowhere to stop for refreshments on this walk so you'll need to carry sufficient food and drink for the day. Don't forget to pack your foul weather gear too, as there is little shelter once you've left the confines of Deepdale Wood.

Barnard Castle is the natural gateway to Teesdale and is the perfect place from which to start a trek into the dale. This historic old town is renowned for its castle and butter market, its cobbled streets and stone-built back alleys, and for its elegant architecture. Original old shop fronts are a particular feature with many dating from the

Victorian period. The unique chateau-like Bowes Museum, and its collection of European furniture, paintings and ceramics, is a major cultural attraction. However, these must all be left behind as you head towards the magnificent River Tees and the delights of the open countryside which await you.

Make your way to the castle, situated at the end of Galgate and behind the Methodist Church at GR049166. Follow the path beside the castle walls, passing the main entrance on your left, and drop down towards the river until you reach a path going off right between the trees. Take this and follow the River Tees upstream towards a very impressive footbridge. Cross the river here but pause to enjoy the excellent views, both looking back towards the ruins of the castle and upstream towards Towler Hill where the farm buildings are just visible high up amongst the trees. This is where the famous landscape painter, Turner is reputed to have painted a view of the Tees and Barnard Castle in 1816. Turner was commissioned by the Lancastrian historian Thomas Dunham Whitaker to submit work for his book *The History of Richmondshire* in 1816. The artist travelled extensively in the region and some of his finest works were based on inspiration drawn from the Teesdale area.

Barnard Castle.

At the far side of the bridge cross over the road and take the footpath directly opposite which takes you through Deepdale Wood. This area was used as a rifle range during the First and Second World Wars, Barnard Castle and district being an important army training ground during these periods. Sir Winston Churchill and Duncan Sandys visited Teesdale to watch troops practice manoeuvres during the Second World War. Nothing remains from those troubled times, all is quiet and serene now with only the sounds of the birds breaking the stillness. In early summer enormous plants of butterbur line the path; tradition has it that these large leaves were used for wrapping butter before it was taken to market. Wild flowers abound amongst the butterbur including campanula and meadowsweet whilst wild roses line the path.

Ignore any tracks going off to the right and keep to the main path, crossing over a ford at one point. Soon you reach a footbridge which takes you onto the other side of the river. Once again follow the obvious path, going over a stile eventually before passing some falls on your right. Shortly afterwards you reach a further stile on your right. Cross over here, dropping down onto a natural stony pavement which was possibly an old river bed. Cross over it and keep in the same general direction before going over a fence and into an open grassy area. Do not ascend the hill but fork right just after passing a solitary tree (the path is very vague at first) and drop down to reach the riverside once more. Soon you reach a stile which gives access to the river – make your way across it (the stones can be slippery at times). Follow the main track as it curves right initially to lead you away from the river before eventually ascending the hillside. Below you the brown waters of Deepdale Beck can be occasionally glimpsed through the trees and a strong smell of wild garlic scents the air.

Eventually an open area is reached which is waist-high in bracken in late summer and where the ground drops steeply away on your left down to the river. Soon we plunge into the trees once more and the path then climbs steeply before reaching the boundary of the wood. The path levels out now as the buildings of Cat Castle Cottages come into view. Shortly after this you pass the remains of an old viaduct on your right.

If you pause here and look across the valley you can just glimpse the sandstone abuttments of the viaduct on the other side. It is hard to conceive of it now but the viaduct, made entirely of iron, spanned this deep valley at a height of 49 metres above the beck; it was named

Cat Castle Bridge after local crags which have now been quarried away. The viaduct, built in the 1860s, was designed by Thomas Bouch for the railway line which went from Barnard Castle to Kirkby Stephen (once the highest railway in England) and was used to transport stone from the quarries for the building of Hury and Blackton Reservoirs.

After another short climb the path emerges at a confusing junction of paths and an open area. Turn right on a vague path to the right of an old tree stump. The cottages can just be glimpsed ahead with the path becoming clearer as you approach the disused railway track. If you turn right at the track bed you can take a look down and across the valley from the edge of the viaduct – but take great care as it could be dangerous. Otherwise turn left and follow the railway track, past the cottages and the entrance to Cat Castle Quarries which have now been re-opened.

After approximately 360 metres (400 yards) we reach metal gates on either side of the old railway track at GR015168; turn through the one on your left and follow the path across the field. (After the confines of the wood it comes as a dramatic change to be walking amongst wide open spaces with unbroken views all around.) In the next field walk half left towards the buildings ahead – there is no visible path so you may find it easier to aim for the stone wall on your left and follow this to the far side of the field. Follow the farm track past The Rigg farmhouse. Keep on in the same direction, passing

Viaduct over Deep Dale Beck, in its heyday. *(National Railway Museum)*

The Butter Stone.

the last of the farm buildings on your left and heading towards a gate ahead and ignoring the stile in the far left corner of the field. For those of you of a nervous disposition, you can dismiss any gunfire heard along here as it undoubtedly originates from the army firing range which you will be passing shortly – at a safe distance, I hasten to add!

Keeping in the same direction of due west, keep on through a series of fields which have gated access (this is a bridleway). Crag Pond can just be glimpsed away to your left, followed by Crag Hill, whilst over to your right are magnificent views along the Teesdale valley and the hills beyond. There's a feeling along here of having attained great height although you are not aware of having climbed significantly since leaving Barnard Castle. Eventually you cross a narrow field. In the following one keep on in the same direction with a wire fence on your right and soon you will see a farm track coming in from the left. Keep straight on until you join it and follow it all the way to the road at GR994166.

Turn right along the road and follow it for approximately 1.6 kilometres (one mile), crossing over Washfold Bridge before passing the army training range of Battle Hill on your left. There is a grass verge beside the road for most of this section. The embankments made for target practice are easily visible from the road whilst Barnard Castle can be seen away to your right in the distance. The road dips down to North Gill Bridge after having passed a road off to the right to Lartington. It then rises out of the gill and once over the brow a footpath sign is reached on your left. At this point there is a choice of routes as the path indicated is non-existent and entails rather a lot of rough ground over Currack Rigg.

For those of you feeling adventurous the route is as follows: take a bearing on Currack Rigg and make your way as best you can amongst the heather. Once over the high ground take another bearing on Booze Wood and drop down to a good track at GR987189 and the entrance to the Rare Breeds Farm. Here you meet up with the alternative route.

ALTERNATIVE ROUTE: Carry on along the road, past a group of Scots Pine trees on your right enclosed by a stone wall. Shortly after this you reach a bridleway sign on your left and 90 metres (100 yards) beyond this another bridleway sign opposite a further group of pine trees. Just ahead of you, also on the left, is a curious boulder called the Butter Stone on the OS map. (This was where during a plague in the seventeenth century, plague victims came to buy dairy produce, including butter; their payment to the farmers was left in jars of vinegar.) Turn left here at this second bridleway sign at GR 990184 and follow the obvious path, contouring Casset How. Eventually you approach a dry stone wall on your right adjacent to High Corn Park. Keep on in the same general direction until you reach several footpath signs and a good track at GR 987189. This is the entrance to Booze

Ruined farm buildings at Briscoe Lane End (before Hury Reservoir).

Hury Reservoir.

Wood Rare Breeds Farm and also where you will meet up with the adventurous souls on the original route – if any!

Walk along the farm track which becomes a tarmac road and follow it all the way to Briscoe Farm. The road is bounded by short cropped grass enabling you to avoid the hard surface (it always pays to consider your feet, especially in hot weather). The flat-topped hill diagonally left of you and reminiscent of Ingleborough in the Yorkshire Dales, is Goldsborough Hill. This is on an alternative section of the Pennine Way which crosses Cotherstone Moor before descending to Blackton Reservoir in Baldersdale. In a little over 1.6 kilometres (a mile) you drop down towards the road at Briscoe Farm, crossing over a beck and a cattle grid before reaching the road at GR978195. Don't be tempted by the lane which comes in from the left immediately after you've crossed the beck.

Turn left along the road and follow it for 1.6 kilometres, passing some strange mounds in the fields on your left, which are mine shafts. Drop down to the bridge over the River Balder, ignoring a road off to the left signed to Hury and Blackton Reservoirs. From the bridge the overflow from Hury Reservoir becomes visible. A steep climb follows to reach a building marked on the 1:25,000 map as Strathmore Arms. Sadly the Strathmore Arms is no more but traces above the doorway can be seen of the original pub sign. My own reactions on reaching this spot on a very hot day are unprintable! Turn left here at the entrance to Hury Reservoir.

Toilets are situated adjacent to a fishing lodge where the fishermen keep a record of their daily catch. There is also a picnic area with tables and this makes a delightful spot for a break with superb views along the length of the reservoir. Goldsborough Hill can be seen again, quite close by this time. This is Hannah Hawkswell country, the lady who captured the hearts of millions in Yorkshire Television's programme *Too Long a Winter* with her courage and natural dignity. She led a primitive existence at Low Birk Hat Farm which is at the far end of Blackton Reservoir, beyond Hury. Since leaving there for a more comfortable situation (which we pass tomorrow), she has become a national celebrity through her regular appearances in the media, especially on television.

Carry on through the car park to the far corner, ignoring the gate on your left which leads down to the side of the reservoir and go instead through the very old iron gate ahead. Follow the sunken lane adjacent to a hedge on your left uphill towards some ruined buildings, passing through a further gate. As you approach the buildings and a metal gate, do not go through the gate but go right, across some rough ground to a stile in the far corner of the field behind a ruined building. Once over here turn right and follow a stone wall on your right all the way uphill to reach a stile in the top right corner of the field. This takes you out onto a road at GR 962200.

Turn right along the road where an impressive vista appears on your right of Baldersdale and Blackton Reservoir is visible over your shoulder. Approximately 360 metres (400 yards) along here a road off to the right is signed to Baldersdale South and just beyond this sign you will find a gate on your left. Pass through here and follow the tractor marks across the field and through the gate ahead. There is a confusion of paths here but keep straight on as the path climbs up through a rocky area which is a small disused quarry. At the top, walk half right towards some trees on the skyline; just before reaching the far corner of the field you meet a stile. Once over this, turn left and follow the wall to its end where it turns sharp left. Keep straight on here in a northerly direction, crossing a broken wall after a few yards, followed by a boggy area. Ascend the hillside ahead and at the top a stile should come into view in the wall ahead.

Cross over the wall and in the following field keep the same direction until two posts in the wall ahead appear slightly to the right and closer together than all the rest. Aim for these – they flank a stile which takes you into a green lane. A glance over your shoulder will give you another opportunity to enjoy the beauties of Teesdale.

This straight, walled track, known as Fell Lane, was set out during the enclosures of the early nineteenth century and rises from the village of Romaldkirk which we will pass through tomorrow. Some of the large rectangular fields on each side of it were used as sources of sandstone for building materials and peat for the villagers' home fires. The rest of the fields were used mostly for growing food for the growing industrial towns, the pasture land being frequently improved with limestone, burnt in kilns nearby.

Prior to the enclosures, a lady known as Grace Scott from Romaldkirk built a turf hut on the moor to escape the seventeenth-century plague. In this she was successful but unfortunately after a while the hut caught fire and she lost her life. The fields are still enclosed but some have reverted back to their original wild state and there's a feeling of remoteness here on Romaldkirk Moor.

Cross over the green lane and through the gate ahead and cross the next field towards a nick on the skyline. When you reach a gully on your right, cross over and walk towards the far right corner of the field.

Now there unfolds a broad and verdant panorama which includes the welcome sight of Middleton-in-Teesdale in the valley bottom backed by Monks Moor, while further to the east we can see Egglestone Common followed by the great expanse of Hamsterley Forest. Middleton Common rises beyond Monks Moor and, to the west, the village of Newbiggin can be seen beyond Middleton, leading the eye on through upper Teesdale. (All of this area has been designated, understandably enough, an Area of Outstanding Natural Beauty.) Crossthwaite Common lies south west of Middleton, with Harter Fell the visible high point directly above an escarpment. Just to the right of this is the ancient mound of Kirkcarrion; this Bronze Age burial mound is a prominent landmark from the centre of Middleton and, indeed, for many miles around. A sepulchral chamber was found here in 1804 complete with a burial urn and the bones of a Brigantine prince – Caryn – hence the name 'Kirkcarrion', meaning 'Caryn's Castle'. Local legend has it that Caryn's unsettled spirit still stalks the fells in the moonlight. Lord Strathmore, father to John Bowes of Bowes Museum, had Scots Pines planted here to mark the spot.

Go over the stile here and drop down in the direction of a clump of trees ahead with Middleton in the distance. Carry on towards a dry-stone wall with a disused quarry far away to your right and passing a fallen and mysterious skeletal structure close by. Turn right along the wall and follow it as it eventually turns left to reach Swarthy Mere Farm. Follow the track past the farm and, as it swings right, go through the gate on your left. (You might like to pause here to envy the farmer his view which he can enjoy every day.)

Drop straight down through the field to a gate at the bottom leading out onto the road. Walk down the road to the T-junction at GR961232 and turn right to follow this minor road for just over 800 metres (½ mile). At this point the houses of Mickleton come into view and you reach a dismantled railway. Cross over the road bridge which crosses the old railway line and turn immediately right through a gate which takes you down to the railway track. Turn right along the track towards Middleton-in-Teesdale.

Unlike many railway tracks this one is not enclosed or claustrophobic but soon becomes elevated, giving superb views across Teesdale towards Monks Moor and beyond. If you can cope with the weight, a pocket guide to wild flowers would be extremely useful along here. Teesdale is rightly famous for its wild flowers and a remarkable number can be found along this stretch; scabious, harebells, orchids and four different species of wild roses were just a few that I spotted one day in high summer.

Soon you reach a minor road which you cross before continuing along the railway track. At this point it takes you along a viaduct which passes high over the River Lune and you can look down on the single-arched road bridge which is an older structure. Carry on along the track until you reach the buildings at Lonton and a footpath sign to Middleton on your right by an old concrete railway stile. (Those of you wishing to camp overnight need to keep on the railway track here until you reach a minor road at GR 952245. Turn left along the road and follow it for just under 800 metres (½ mile) until the road bends right. Follow it round and the camp site is just round the corner on the right. The site was originally Middleton's old railway station.)

Otherwise take the stile on your right, passing between a farm house and a barn conversion and aim for a stile in the far left hand

Middleton House, Middleton.

corner of the field. Turn left along the road for a few metres until you reach a footpath sign and a stile on your right. Go over here and follow the obvious path which goes diagonally left across the field and then over a stile in the corner. Drop down across the corner of the next field in the same direction to a stone stile which takes you into the trees. Carry on along an obvious path down to a gate and stile in the far corner. This takes you to the river bank and you finish the day as you started, by the banks of the mighty Tees. You soon join up with a good farm track which leads to the road.

However, prior to reaching the road is a path off to your right which cuts the corner off and leads to a stile which gives access to the road. Turn right here and follow the road up into the middle of the town. As you reach the T-junction at the top, spare a minute or two to look at the water fountain on your right-hand side. This was erected in 1877 by R. W. Bainbridge in memory of his long service with The London Lead Company. This is the spot where most walks start and finish in the town.

Middleton-in-Teesdale has several pubs, a hotel, shops and B&B accommodation as well as the camp site mentioned earlier. It is a fascinating town, often referred to as the capital of Upper Teesdale and full of buildings of architectural interest relating to the lead mining industry.

In 1815 the London Lead Mining Company bought an estate in

Middleton and during the next 100 years it was transformed into a boom town where lead was more important than gold. The Quaker Company, as it was more commonly known, moved its headquarters here in 1880 and built practically every nineteenth-century building in the town. They ran schools, libraries, horticultural societies, mechanics' institutes, bath houses etc. all for the benefit of the workers and also introduced the railway to Middleton in 1868.

As the population increased so did the tradesmen and by 1827 Middleton had 2 blacksmiths, 6 carriers, 2 butchers, 4 surgeons, 5 tailors, 2 strawhat and dressmakers, 3 stonemasons, 4 joiners, 14 grocers and drapers, 4 academies or private schools, 2 clock and watch-makers, and 2 clog makers – oh, and 6 inns!

Buildings of particular interest include the Superintendent's House (Middleton House) which lies at the far end of the town on the Hude, past the old corn mill. The yard adjacent to the house encompasses a clocktower which is beautifully built in the Company's style and can be seen from the market place. The model housing estate of Masterman Place, east of the town, was built in 1824 to house co-workers. The company also established a 'Ready Money Shop' which is now the Trustee Savings Bank. It was known as 'The Governor and Company's Teesdale Workman's Corn Association' and is thought to be the world's first Cooperative store. (It vies with Rochdale for this distinction.) Perhaps the most memorable piece of architecture is the drinking fountain which you passed on your way in. This was erected by R. W. Bainbridge, who was retiring as the superintendent of the London Lead Company and would have lived in Middleton House, just mentioned. The fountain is a superb example of ornate Victorian ironwork.

The Parish Church of St Mary is close to the site of a thirteenth-century one built in the Decorated style. Unfortunately this was destroyed about 1880 by the Revd Milner who wanted it replaced with a larger building. Items from the thirteenth-century church can be found inside the present one and include a piscina and the pedestal to the font. In the church yard can be seen a re-erected East Window from the Decorated church and also a sixteenth-century bell tower which is the only detached one in the county.

Middleton is also an ideal spot to start an exploration of the upper dale and the remote moorland beyond. It is particularly famous for its waterfalls which include Low and High Force and Cauldron Snout – the latter being one of England's longest and largest cataracts. The area north west of Middleton is part of Upper Teesdale National Nature Reserve which protects many rare species of flowers and is also an AONB (Area of Oustanding Natural Beauty). It has much to offer the visitor with time to spare and a desire to explore this unique region.

The drinking fountain at
Middleton-in-Teesdale.

Walk 5

Day Two
Middleton-in-Teesdale to Barnard Castle

Distance 18.4 kms (11.5 miles)
Ordnance Survey Map
1:25,000
    Outdoor Leisure 31 – Teesdale
1:50,000
    Landranger 92 – Barnard Castle & Richmond

*M*iddleton is left behind through delightful wild flower meadows, followed by an easy undulating stroll by the River Tees which entices us on through a number of idyllic villages: Egglestone with its Georgian houses and medieval field systems; the picturesque Romaldkirk which can boast three village greens complete with Victorian pumps and an even older set of village stocks; Cotherstone, famous for its cheese and at least one celebrated resident and finally, Lartington and its delightful old cottages and topiary. The day finishes as it started, beside the Tees, and as you cross the foot-bridge to reach Barnard Castle you can revisit the picturesque view of the castle which has been painted by so many artists down the ages.

Leave Middleton by the drinking fountain, walking due east on the B6282 towards Egglestone. After approximately 450 metres (500 yards) the main road bends away to the left as you reach a school on your right. Keep straight on here along Leekworth Gardens and where Meadow Close curves away left keep straight on along the narrowing lane. Take the stile to the right of the gate ahead which takes you into open fields. Carry on along an obvious path a short distance away from a wall and hedge on your left, keeping straight on when the wall turns sharp left. Go over the stile in the stone wall ahead and cross a further field and stile. In the following field keep in the same direction through a line of trees beside a beck. The relative hustle and bustle of Middleton is left behind and you're amid beautiful scenery once more as you walk through meadows which are full of wild flowers in high summer.

Once through the trees, keep the same direction across the next field to a further belt of trees. Follow the waymarks here as the path has been diverted, turning right along the edge of the trees to a stile in the wall ahead. Once over this, fork left to enter the woodland where you should encounter a seat in memory of Frank Lockwood. A series of steps takes you down to a bridge over a beck and then to the riverside. The walking is delightful here amongst the trees along an obvious path as we follow the Tees downstream for approximately 1.6 kilometres (1 mile). Duckboards are conveniently positioned over some rather damp sections.

Whilst first walking along this stretch I came upon an Alder tree which had been invaded by some form of caterpillar which was gradually killing it. The whole tree was covered in finely woven webs reminiscent of a shroud, even the trunk had been encased with delicate webbing. The bank on your left is a haven for rabbits.

After its initial undulations the path now levels out and the majestic Tees flows deep and wide beside it. After passing the remains of an old quarry at GR976246 the path leaves the river bank (this is way-marked) and climbs uphill. The village of Mickleton can be seen on the right over the other side of the river. Keep on this broad track, joining up with a concrete road coming in from the right from Ornella Farm and follow this all the way to the road.

At the main road take great care and cross over, following the road straight ahead signed to Blackton & Stanhope. Follow the road for just under 800 metres (½ mile), passing Eggleston Baptist Church en route. Eventually you reach the entrance to Toft House on the right followed by a Teesdale Way sign – follow this down to the ford. If the water is too deep you can use the bridge which is off to the right.

Follow the track across a further stream – there is a foot-bridge on your left if needed, and carry on up a slight rise to a crossing of tracks. Go straight over here, following the Teesdale Way sign. When you reach the main entrance to a large stone house on your left, turn right through an old gateway. Walk diagonally left to a stile in the wall ahead. Keep straight on with a wall on your left to reach a rough

track coming in from the right. There are wonderful views here along
the length of Teesdale once more. At the end of the field pass through
a gateway and keep straight on with the wall on your left. Follow the
path as it eventually drops down right to meet another rough track
coming in from the right at a gateway.

You are walking on ground rich in ancient history in this field which
is known as Side Riggs; note the steepness of the ground. The field was
formally known as 'The Linces', which translates from an old English
word 'Linc' meaning a bank. These strip lynchets, or ploughing
terraces, enabled the Anglian farmers to cultivate crops on ground
which would otherwise have been unproductive. The early ploughs
were usually pulled by oxen and on sloping ground it would be
impossible to prevent the plough from periodically swinging downhill.

The path is obvious all the way to the road at GR999237. As you
reach the houses of Egglestone, drop down through a belt of trees
beside a beck, ignoring a path which goes slightly higher leading to a
metal gate marked Private. In the final field adjacent to the church a
stile will be seen in the wall on your left which takes you out onto
a track. Follow this right, into the centre of Egglestone. On the
opposite side of the village green is a shop whilst just up the road to
your left is the Three Tuns Inn.

The village green was originally much larger and extended all the way
down to the old chapel close to the Tees. A stream from the moor
top, which became culverted, ran straight down the centre of the
green. During times of strife the villagers led their animals onto the
green and haycocks were used to block up the spaces left between
the houses. Egglestone was the centre for smelting in the dale during
the height of the mining period. The mill was at Blackton, just 1½
kilometres away up the moor road. Its accompanying chimney lasted
until 1932 when it was demolished by Tom Allinson, one of the last
lead miners, amidst great cheering from the huge crowd which had
gathered. The ruins of the twelfth-century Egglestone Abbey is several
miles away on the other side of Barnard Castle and was founded by
the 'White Canons', so named because of the colour of their robes.

Turn right to reach the B6282 and then left along it, keeping to the
footpath until you reach a junction. Turn right here, following the
road signed to Romaldkirk, down to Egglestone Bridge. The entrance

Egglestone Bridge.

to Egglestone Hall & Gardens is passed on your right and if you cross the road at this point you pass Hell Beck cascading over a natural amphitheatre of rocks. The bridge overhead is owned by Egglestone Hall and links one part of their grounds to another.

Cross over Egglestone Bridge, which is an impressive double-arched structure, thought to be seventeenth, or even fifteenth century in origin; a chapel existed on the bridge at one time. Collingwood Mill stood on the north side of the bridge and was a corn mill for the village of Romaldkirk, in use until 1870. The mill race can be seen at low water and discarded millstones have been discovered; of the mill itself, though, there is nothing left. As you start to climb the hill you reach a sign on your left to the Teesdale Way, follow this on a broad grassy path as it rises towards the trees. Egglestone Hall comes into view on the left, completed in 1820 and consisting of two projecting wings with the main entrance sporting a single-storey Grecian colonnade. The hall was a finishing school for girls and became famous for its Flower School. The four acres of organic gardens are a flower-arranger's paradise and are open to the public all year.

Walk up the hill, keeping a short distance from the fence and woodland on your left. The wire fence soon gives way to a breeze-block wall which comes as quite a shock in this pastoral location; fortunately, nature is having her way and the wall is slowly becoming encrusted with lichens and mosses. Hewcroft Hill, which you are now ascending, was the burial site for the plague victims in 1644. Follow the wall to a stile in the top corner of the field. Once over, walk diagonally left towards a telegraph pole on the skyline – 160° – gradually leaving the woodland on your left, until you reach a stile in the corner. Turn right over the stile and walk towards the village of Romaldkirk which can be seen ahead. After passing a graveyard over to your right, leave the main track and walk diagonally left towards the trees. Go over a stile in front of the trees and turn right to follow a good path which takes you into the village. Turn right on reaching the road, passing Romaldkirk House on the right which is the old rectory. Opposite this building is Low Green containing one of the village's two Victorian pumps. When you reach the road junction opposite the Kirk Inn your route lies to the left but you will doubtless spare some time to wander around this beautiful village.

On your right lies the twelfth-century parish church of St Romald, known as the Cathedral of the Dales. The decorative tower clock face was erected to commemorate Queen Victoria's Diamond Jubilee in 1897. The church contains some Saxon stonework and also pre-Reformation frescoes on the west end pillars. It is well worth a visit and handy notes are set up beside the items of special interest.

Romaldkirk has been inhabited since Roman times and has with-

Romaldkirk.

stood devastation by William the Conqueror and marauding Scots. It has three village greens, the middle one of which was originally cobbled and railed and it is here that the village stocks can be found. High Green further along contains the second of the village pumps and is dated 1866. The village hall was built 'To the Memory of King Edward VII' and has a conifer tree adjacent to it, surrounded by steps. This marks the site of a large sycamore tree known as the Toby Tree, upon which public notices were displayed. It was so named after Tobias Bayles who died in 1652.

After looking around the village retrace your steps to the crossroads by the village church and, with the Kirk Inn on your right, turn right towards two houses. Take the track between the two, following a Teesdale Way sign. At the end of this path go through the left one of two gates, beneath some trees and then walk towards a radio mast ahead, which is half-left. Soon the path becomes visible and leads to a gate. Go through into the next field in the same direction to a gap in the hedge ahead. Go through the squeeze stile here and drop down onto a good track coming in from the right to reach the ruins at Low Garth. Ignore the Teesdale Way sign directing you left and go over the stile here and follow the hedge on your right to cross over a further stile at the end of the field. Follow the obvious path through the meadow to another squeeze stile and then uphill to reach a gate. Turn left and follow the line of the fence, ignoring the path which contours the hillside. Along here you will pass an unusual stone building which has a blocked, arched window. This is reputed to have been the resting place of monks travelling between Egglestone Abbey and Romaldkirk.

Go through the gateway ahead, across the next field to the extreme far corner and a stile beside a gate. The Teesdale Way rejoins you here, coming in on a broad track from the left. Follow the track up towards Woden Croft. The River Tees is far below with high cliffs on the far side. This area was the scene of the death of the last Lord Romaldkirk who was killed whilst out hunting a white deer at nightfall. An old lady had warned him to go home but he paid her no heed and fell to his death on the brink of Percy Mere. (There's a moral there somewhere ...)

Once you reach the buildings of Woden Croft, follow the waymarks passing in front of the houses, turning left after passing the last house and following the track back towards the river. Woden Croft is reputedly one of the 'Yorkshire Schools' which Charles Dickens exposed in his novel Nicholas Nickleby. Richard Cobden, founder of the Anti-Corn Law League, attended Woden Croft and because of his experiences there he could never afterwards endure to speak of it.

Pass through the gate at the far end of the field following a high wall on your right. (This enclosed area contains the summerhouse belonging to Woden Croft, an attractive stone building sporting a carved inscription and a sundial; this area is private, however.) A look to the left along here will give a dramatic glimpse of the peaty brown waters of the Tees rushing along far below, flanked by the high cliffs. Keep on the main path which runs across the centre of the next field and as you descend, ignore the tractor path which curves away right over a stream and keep straight on. Soon you reach a fence edging the woodland, follow this to a little stream. The official right of way goes over a stile in the fence on your left here, crosses the stream and follows the fence for a short stretch before crossing back over! However there is a well used path over the stream ahead, which joins up with the official route – the choice is yours. Keep on alongside

The 'Monks Resting Place'.

Summerhouse, Woden Croft.

the fence. At the end of the field a stile takes you into the woodland and down to the Tees.

The path now follows the river downstream towards Cotherstone. (In high summer the smell of wild garlic assaults the nostrils or delights the senses, depending on your taste.) Keep on this side of the river, ignoring a foot-bridge which crosses the Tees. Eventually you reach a footbridge taking you over the river Balder (named after a Viking god) coming in from the right. Notice the modern iron boundary marker inscribed 'Cotherstone' at each end of the foot-bridge; similar sculptures can be seen along the Teesdale Way and mark the 12 Parish boundaries. You will see more of them later.

Follow the path directly in front of you marked Teesdale Way, up the steep grassy hill ahead to a fork in the path. Turn left here (the path to the right is too narrow) and follow the path until you reach a broad track along which we turn right. Cotherstone Castle once stood in the field on your right, but nothing remains today apart from the mound and some broken stones. This twelfth-century medieval castle on Hallgarth Hill was the home of Lord Romaldkirk, the last of the Fitzhugh's, who died so tragically. On reaching a building, turn right, passing Hallgarth Hill House.

Records of 1832 show that this beautiful stone building with a superb sundial over the door was once owned by Mr Hutchinson who also owned the field containing the castle ruins. Did the sundial and the pediment, also above the door, originate from the castle I wonder?

> Shortly after this a football field can be seen below you on the right – this area was once common ground known as The Hagg. Soon you reach a tarmac road coming up from the right, follow this uphill to reach the village of Cotherstone. Turn left at the top and follow the road through the village.

Cotherstone has two pubs and a shop, a far cry from the 12 shops, 2 boot and shoe makers, 2 blacksmiths and 3 carpenters in the village at the beginning of this century. The soft crumbly cheese for which the village is famous is still made locally and equally famous is one of its inhabitants, Hannah Hawkswell, as noted earlier. Local stone was

Above: The mausoleum at Lartington.

Left: Hallgarth Hill House, Cotherstone.

used for many of the houses, which was brought from the moor under the Common Rights Act. Often, older buildings were thatched with heather or ling which was collected on Cotherstone Moor. This was very dark in colour and became known as 'black thatch'. The village has now been designated a conservation area in order to help protect its character.

> Keep on through the village, passing the Junior and Infants School on the right, followed by the village green. Follow the road left at a fork, signed to Barnard Castle. Just round the corner is a good track on your left immediately after a wall-mounted post box. This is known as Mire Lane but not marked as such. Follow this to the end and pass through a gate. Continue, following a stone wall on your right to its end at GR 019191. Go over the stile on the right and follow the fence on your left, soon crossing a broken down wall. Half-way up the hill you reach a squeeze stile in the fence on the left. Once through, walk diagonally uphill towards a telegraph pole. After passing the pole on your left you will see a stile ahead. Go over this and walk diagonally left towards the edge of a group of trees, passing by an old gatepost beside them. Go diagonally right across the field towards a raised area in the far corner which leads up to a railway embankment. Take the bridge over the old line and follow the directional arrow across the field towards a further railway bridge. The railway line here is part of the line which you passed yesterday at Cat Castle Cottages. After passing under the line follow the path out onto a lane. Turn right here to reach an ancient graveyard on your right.

There is a wonderfully elaborate grave on the right as you pass through the gates; it is dated 1897 and consists of a canopy raised on decorative pillars complete with capitals. This is a Roman Catholic cemetery containing the family mausoleum once belonging to Lartington Hall.

> If you've time on your hands to visit the tiny village of Lartington then bear right past the graveyard to reach the main street.

Lartington was originally built as an estate village and possesses some quaint cottages. Like Cotherstone it is designated a Conservation area and ten of its cottages are listed. The Clock House is the former village school of the early nineteenth century. However, recent renovations show that part at least may date from the 1590s. The gardens of the cottages are as fascinating as the houses and include some

intricate topiary and a knot garden. At the far end of the village where
the road goes over the old railway line is a view of The Woodlands,
a Victorian stone building with elaborate chimneys which was once
the old railway station. As you retrace your steps along the street look
out for a magnificent stone cross inscribed I.H.S. on the other side
of the road. This overlooks the village pond on its far side and was
once the centre of the village green. Make your way back to the
graveyard and turn right following the waymarks beneath the yew
trees.

OTHERWISE follow the waymarks on your left almost directly opposite the entrance to the graveyard, going beneath some ancient
yew trees and passing a Victorian iron signpost directing you to Barnard
Castle and painted black and white. Soon Lartington Hall comes into
view on your right. The present hall was built during the reign of
King Charles I in the early seventeenth century and has been greatly
extended over the years. The park was extended with lakes, shelter
belts and waterfalls. Formal gardens, a terrace and a ha-ha were
constructed in front of the hall whilst behind it was built the family
mausoleum and cemetery which you have just passed. The park is
used annually as the site for the Teesdale County Fair.

Lartington.

Go over the stile at the edge of the trees and walk diagonally left towards a monkey-puzzle tree containing a waymark. Ahead of you are some interesting gardens belonging to Home Farm. Just beyond the ancient tree you reach a stile in the iron fence ahead. Go over here and drop down left over a little stream to reach the banks of Scur Beck. Don't take the foot-bridge across the beck but turn right and follow its southern bank beneath Grotto Wood. This is beautiful walking along here with rhododendrons edging the wood and Scur Beck scurrying along beneath. Mimulus can be seen growing on a little outcrop in the beck and the whole area is surrounded by mature parkland belonging to the Lartington Hall Estate. Soon you reach a road where you turn left and follow it round to the buildings at Pecknell. At the T-junction turn right. To your left is a camp-site surrounded by very old barns with crumbling roofs, one of the barns is dated 1866.

Go through the gate ahead and keep straight on towards a house. Follow the directional arrows round to the left of the building and keep on along a good path across the field to a gate. This leads you into Pecknell Wood. After a few metres you join the main track coming in from your left and you drop down eventually to a house, after a bend in the track. This is where I was once amazed to see a peacock perched on the apex of the front porch of Teesbridge Cottage as if posing for a photograph. Soon after this you cross over a beck and should spot two more of the boundary sculptures, this time marked 'Lartington'. Eventually you emerge from the woods into parkland and after reaching the end of a belt of trees the ruins of Barnard Castle come into view. Follow the track out onto the B6277 and turn left and then left again to reach the foot-bridge over the Tees which you crossed only yesterday. Turn right on the far bank and retrace your steps to the castle ruins. Turn left by the castle walls and follow the path up the hill to the centre of Barnard Castle.

There is every amenity in the town and so much to see you'll wish you had more time to spare. There is an abundance of cafés and pubs in which you can toast your completion of Barney's Round. Alternatively the local Tourist Information Centre can provide plenty of guidance for those of you with time to explore this historic town and the surrounding area.

The castle itself was built in the twelfth century by Bernard Baliol on a rock overlooking the Tees; the town gradually grew up around it and was named after him. The massive curtain walls still remain, enclosing a park-like area which was used for safety in times of danger. The Round Tower, with its spiral stone vaulting, arrow slits and spiral staircases within, which was built about 1200, is perhaps the most interesting part of all. This tower commands superb views up the river and can itself be seen for many miles around.

Barnard Castle, known locally as Barney, lies on the course of a Roman road which crossed the River Tees by a ford 120 metres upstream from the castle. County Bridge, which lies below the castle walls, was repaired in 1569 but may be of thirteenth-century origin. It once spanned the boundaries between Yorkshire and Durham. Illicit weddings were conducted in the centre of the bridge in a tiny chapel which is shown in some old engravings. These were performed by Cuthbert Hilton (a bible clerk) for half-a-crown – some of us can still remember this old currency!

The Butter Market (known locally as the Market Cross) is an octagonal building built in 1747 as a town hall. This famous landmark

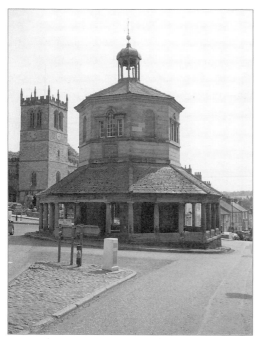

The Butter Market at Barnard Castle.

has had a variety of uses over the years including a store for local butter which was kept cool there. The veranda encircling the building was used for the sale of milk, cheese and of course butter. There's a story that in 1804 two men stepped out of a nearby inn to settle a dispute regarding their firing abilities. They both took aim at the weather vane on top of the cross and the bullet holes can still be seen today.

The French-style chateau of Bowes Museum, which stands just outside the town, looks totally out of character with the surrounding countryside but you can't fail to be impressed by this magnificent edifice. It was built by John Bowes of Streatlam Castle, (son of the 10th Earl of Strathmore) and his wife Josephine, a French actress, to house their vast collection of European furniture, pictures and ceramics. Constructed between 1869 and 1875, its costs escalated by three times the original estimate of £38,500; sadly neither John Bowes nor his wife lived to see it finished. The museum is now in the hands of Durham County Council and its collections are among the most important in the country.

Oliver Cromwell is reputed to have stayed in Blagraves House, one of the oldest buildings in the area. The present building dates from the early sixteenth century although the cellars and a secret passage are of even earlier origin. It is situated close to the Butter Market and is currently a restaurant. Other famous people to have visited the area include Charles Dickens and Sir Walter Scott. Dickens stayed at the King's Head in the market place whilst researching into the notorious Yorkshire schools for his novel Nicholas Nickleby, whilst the scenery, folklore and history of the area inspired Sir Walter Scott to write his romantic poem *Rokeby*. He stayed with his friend John Morritt, the owner of Rokeby Park, on two occasions and retreated to a cave overlooking the River Greta to write his famous poem. Artists too have been drawn to the beautiful landscapes surrounding Barnard Castle and the River Tees. John Sell Cotman and Joseph Turner are the most famous of these.

Date walked _____

Companions _____
_____
_____

Weather _____

Highlight of the walk _____
_____
_____
_____

Any other memories _____
_____
_____

Blagraves House, Barnard Castle.

Additional Information

WALK 1: ALSTON REEL

Alston Tourist Information Centre, The Railway Station, Alston, Cumbria CA9 3JB (01434 381696)

Alston half-day closing – Tuesday.
Nenthead P.O. closes early Tuesday.

Hostels:

Alston Youth Hostel, The Firs, Alston, Cumbria CA9 3RW (01434 381509).

Ninebanks Youth Hostel, Orchard House, Mohope, Ninebanks, Hexham, Northumberland (01434 345288).

Camp Site:

Tyne Willow Site, Moredun Garage, Alston, Cumbria (01434 381318).

Bunkhouses:

The Miners Arms, Nenthead, Alston, Cumbria CA9 3PF (01434 381427).

Mill Cottage Bunkhouse, Nenthead Mines Heritage Centre, Nenthead, Alston, Cumbria CA9 3PD (01434 382037).

B&Bs:

Mrs V. Thompson, 'Nentholme', The Butts, Alston CA9 3JQ (01434 381523).

Mrs J. Best, Chapel House, Alston CA9 3SH (01434 381112).

Blueberry's Teashop & Guesthouse, Market Place, Alston CA9 3QN (01434 381928).

Mrs Armstrong, Foulardrigg, Nenthead, Alston CA9 3LP (01434 382609).

Mrs H. Sherlock, Cherry Tree, Nenthead, Alston CA9 3PD (01434 381434/382368).

Crown Inn, Nenthead, Alston, Cumbria (01434 381271).

The Miners Arms, Nenthead, Alston, Cumbria CA9 3PF (01434 381427).

Miscellaneous:

The Pennine Pottery, Clargillhead House, Alston, Cumbria CA9 3NG (01434 382157).

Nenthead Mines Heritage Centre, Nenthead, Alston, Cumbria CA9 3PD (01434 382037).

Thortergill Tea Rooms, the Johnston Family, Thortergill, Garrigill, Alston, Cumbria CA9 3DH (01434 381936).

Transport:

Alston Taxis: 01434 381386.

Regional Railways North East Ltd: 0345 484950, for details of trains between Hexham & Haltwhistle.

Cumbria Travel Information, and Northumberland Travel Information: 01228 606000.

For details of buses to Alston from Carlisle and Newcastle, and also buses to Nenthead: 01670 533128.

WALK 2: ALLENDALE AMBLE

Haltwhistle Tourist Information Centre, Church Hall, Main St, Haltwhistle, Northumberland NE49 0BE (01434 322002).

Hexham Tourist Information Centre, The Manor Office, Hallgate, Hexham, Northumberland NE46 1XD (01434 605225).

Haltwhistle half-day closing – Wednesday.
Allendale Town – none.
Hexham half-day closing – Thursday.

Hostels:

Once Brewed Youth Hostel, Military Rd, Bardon Mill, Hexham, Northumberland NE47 7AN (01434 344360).

Acomb Youth Hostel, Main St, Acomb, Hexham, Northumberland NE46 4PL (01434 602864).

Camp Sites:

Haltwhistle Camping & Caravanning Club Site, Burnfoot, Haltwhistle NE49 0HZ (01434 320106). 3.2 kms (2 miles) from Haltwhistle.

Seldom Seen Caravan Park, Haltwhistle (01434 320571). Backpackers only.

Riverside Leisure, Tyne Green Rd, Hexham (01434 604705).

Causey Hill Caravan Park, Hexham (01434 602834).

B&Bs:

Mrs S. Barwick, Allendale Tea Rooms, Market Place, Allendale Town, Hexham, Northumberland (01434 683575).

Thornley House, Allendale, Hexham, Northumberland NE47 9NH (01434 683255).

Alan & Carol Davison, Oakeydene, Allendale, Hexham, Northumberland (01434 683572). 1.6 kms (1 mile) out of Allendale Town on the Whitfield Road (owners will provide transport into

Allendale Town for evening meal and also to regain route the following day).

Struthers Farm, Catton, Allendale, Hexham, Northumberland NE47 9LP (01434 683580). On the route, 3.2 km (2 miles) short of Allendale Town (camping is a possibility if you phone first).

Heather Coulson, The Old Hostel, 1 Allen View, Catton, Allendale, Hexham, Northumberland (01434 683780). 1km (¾ mile) off route and 2.4 kms (1½ miles) short of Allendale Town.

For B&Bs in Haltwhistle and Hexham contact the Tourist Information Centres.

King's Head Hotel, Market Place, Allendale Town, Hexham, Northumberland NE47 9BD (01434 683 681).

Hare & Hounds Hotel, Allendale Town, Hexham, Northumberland (01434 683300).

Miscellaneous:

Vindolanda, Bardon Mill, Hexham, Northumberland NE47 7JN (01434 344277).

Transport:

Hexham based: Carr's Taxis, 01434 603824.

Allendale Town: Dave Wilson, 01434 683663.

Haltwhistle: Bainbridge, 01434 320515.

Regional Railways North East Ltd: 0345 484950, for details of trains between Hexham and Haltwhistle.

Northumberland Transport Information: 01670 533128, for details of buses between Hexham and Haltwhistle and Allendale Town.

A bus service also runs along the Roman wall in the summer months.

WALK 3: MERLINS WAY

Stanhope Tourist Information Centre, Durham Dales Centre Ltd, Castle Gardens, Stanhope, Weardale, Co. Durham DL13 2FJ (01388 527650/526393).

Stanhope half-day closing – none.
Edmundbyers – Village shop open every day. Lunch 12.30–2.0.

Hostels:

Youth Hostel, Edmundbyers, Low House, Edmundbyers, Consett, Co. Durham DH8 9NL (01207 255651).

Camp Sites:

Struthers Farm, Edmundbyers, Consett, Co. Durham (01207 255236). This is on the route.

The Eilands, Landieu, Frosterley, Weardale, Co. Durham DL13 2SJ (01388 527230). This is on the route.

Heather View Caravan Park, Stanhope, Weardale, Co. Durham (01388 528728). Backpackers only and on the route, 2 kms. (½ mile) from Stanhope.

B&Bs:

Heatherside, Edmundbyers, Consett, Co. Durham DH8 9NL (01207 55674). Centre of village.

Mrs B. Brown, The Burnside, Edmundbyers, Consett DH8 9NG (01207 255257).

Red Lodge Cottage, 2 Market Place, Stanhope, Weardale (01388 527851)

Punch Bowl Inn, Edmundbyers, Consett, Co. Durham (01207 255206).

The Pack Horse Inn, Market Place, Stanhope, Weardale (01388 528407).

The Bonny Moor Hen, Front St, Stanhope, Weardale (01388 528214).

The Queen's Head, Front St, Stanhope, Weardale (01388 528160).

The Lord Crewe Arms Hotel, Blanchland, Co. Durham DH8 9SP (01434 675251).

Transport:

Weardale Private Hire: 01388 527272.

Durham Transport Information: 0191 3833337, for details of buses to Edmundbyers from Consett and also routes along Weardale to Stanhope.

WALK 4: MELMERBY MEANDER

Penrith Tourist Information Centre, Robinson's School, Middlegate, Cumbria CA11 7PT (01768 67466).

Lazonby – half day closing – None.
Melmerby – None.

Camp sites:

Lazonby & Dist. Swimming Pool Ass., Camp Site, Lazonby, Penrith. Secretary, Diane Morgan on 01931 712470.

Site open Easter - Oct. (Free use of pool, open June - Aug.)

Bookings for Camp Site can also be made through the landlord of the Joiners Arms Lazonby (01768 898728).

Melmerby Caravan Park, Melmerby, Penrith, Cumbria CA10 1HE (01768 881311). Limited space so phone ahead.

Thacka Lea Caravan Park, Thacka Lane, Penrith, Cumbria CA11 9HX (01768 63319).

Bunkhouse:

Camping Barn conversion approved January '98 at Busk Rigg Farm, Renwick. For future details enquire at the Tourist Information Centre.

B&Bs:

Gale Hall Farm, Melmerby, Penrith, Cumbria CA10 1HN (01768 881254).

Edith James, Greenholme, Melmerby, Penrith, Cumbria (01768 881436).

Mrs Moreton, Meadowbank, Melmerby, Penrith, Cumbria (01768 881652).

The Joiners Arms, Lazonby, Penrith, Cumbria CA10 1BL (01768 898728).

Banktop House Lazonby, Penrith, Cumbria CA10 1AQ (01768 898268).

The Crown Inn, Kirkoswald, Penrith, Cumbria (01768 898435).

Scale Houses Farm, Scalehouses, Renwick (01768 896493).

Horse & Jockey, Renwick (01768 898579).

Miscellaneous:

The Village Bakery, Melmerby, Penrith, Cumbria CA10 1HE (01768 881515).

Little Salkeld Watermill, Little Salkeld, Penrith, Cumbria CA10 1NN (01768 881523).

Transport:

Lakeland Taxis: (01768 65722).

Regional Railways North East Ltd: 0345 484950 for details of trains to Lazonby.

Cumbria Transport Information: 01228 606000 for details of buses to Lazonby and Melmerby.

WALK 5: BARNEY'S ROUND

Barnard Castle Tourist Information Centre, 43 Galgate, Barnard Castle, Co. Durham DLI2 8EL (01833 690909).

Baldersdale Youth Hostel, Blackton, Baldersdale, Barnard Castle, Co. Durham DLI2 9UP (01833 650629).

Barnard Castle Half-day Closing – Thursday.
Middleton-in-Teesdale Half-day Closing – Wednesday.

Camp Sites:

Daleview Caravan Park, Middleton-in-Teesdale (01833 640233).

Lartington Camping Barn and Camp Site, Pecknell Farm, Lartington, Barnard Castle, Co. Durham DLI2 9DF (01833 638357). 3.2 kms (2 miles) from Barnard Castle.

Dockenflatts Lane Camping and Caravan Site, Lartington, Barnard Castle, Co. Durham DLI2 9DG (01833 630228). Operated by Camping and Caravan Club. 2.4kms (1.5miles) west of Barnard Castle.

Bunkhouses:

Kingsway Adventure Centre, Alston Rd, Middleton-in-Teesdale (01833 640881).

Hudeway Outdoor Centre, Hudeway Farm East, Stacks Lane, Middleton-in-Teesdale (01833 640012).

B&Bs:

For Barnard Castle and Middleton-in-Tees contact the Tourist Information Centre.

Miscellaneous:

Barnard Castle: 01833 638212.

Bowes Museum, Barnard Castle, Co. Durham DLI2 8NP (01833 690606)

Transport:

A&B Taxis: (01833 637766)

Cumbria Transport Information: 01228 606000

Durham Transport Information: 0191 3833337, for details of buses to Barnard Castle and Middleton-in-Teesdale.

GENERAL INFORMATION

Regional Railways North East Ltd: (0345 484950) for details of rail services to Carlisle and Newcastle.

County rail & bus services:

Durham: 0191 3833337
Cumbria: 01228 606000
Northumberland: 01670 533128

Killhope Lead Mining Centre, Weardale (01388 537505).

East Cumbria Countryside Project, Unit 2c, The Old Mill, Warwick Bridge, Carlisle, Cumbria CA4 8RR (01228 561601).

Long Distance Walkers Association, Membership Secretary, Janet Chapman, 63 Yockley Close, The Maultway, Camberley, Surrey GU15 1QQ (01276 65169).

Ramblers Association, 1–5, Wandsworth Road, London SW8 2XX (0171 5826878).

Youth Hostels Association, Trevelyan House, St. Albans, Herts. AL1 2DY (01727 855215).

Ordnance Survey, Romsey Road, Maybush, Southampton, Hants. SO9 4DH (01703 792000).

Selected Bibliography

BARKER, J., *Adventuring into the Allendales*
Peter Robson (Print) Ltd
Hexham 1990

BARKER, J., *Cumbria*
John Bartholomew & Son Ltd
Edinburgh 1977

BELLAMY, D., & QUAYLE, B., *England's Last Wilderness*
Boxtree Ltd
London 1992

CHAPMAN, V., *Pamphlets on Eggleston, Romaldkirk, Cotherstone and Lartington*
High Force

COGGINS, D., *Teesdale in old Photographs*
Alan Sutton Publishing Ltd
Stroud 1990

DILLON, P., *Walking in the North Pennines*
Cicerone Press
Cumbria 1991

DINGWALL, P., *Eden Valley*
Discovery Publishing (UK) Ltd
Middleton-in-Teesdale

EMETT, C., *The Eden Way*
Cicerone Press
Cumbria 1990

FREETHY, R. & M., *Discovering the Pennines*
John Donald Ltd
Edinburgh 1992

GORDON, I. & A., *Settle to Carlisle Walk*
Dalesman Publication 1990

GREAVES, N., *Discovering the Pennines*
The Crowood Press Ltd
Wiltshire 1991

HOLE, C., *British Folk Customs*
Book Club Associates 1976 by arrangement with
Hutchinson Publishing Ltd. London.

LOFTHOUSE, J., *Countrygoers North*
Robert Hale Ltd
London 1965

MITCHELL, W. R., *Wild Pennines*
Robert Hale & Co.
London 1976

PALMER, W. T., *Wanderings in the Pennines*
Skeffington & Son Ltd
London 1951

PARKER, M., & TALLENTIRE, L., *Teesdale and
the High Pennines*
Discovery Guides

SCHOLES, R., *Walking in Eden*
Sigma Leisure 1997

STOREY, T., *Haltwhistle & South Tynedale*
Cameo Books 1973

WATSON, K., *North Country Walks 2*
The Northern Echo Darlington

WELSH, F., *The Companion Guide to the Lake District*
Collins. London 1989

In addition there are various local pamphlets and in particular those published by the East Cumbria Countryside Project group.

Notes